The **Teacher's Essential Guide** Series

Jim Burke

Effective Instruction

How to:

- Use Assessment to Improve Instruction
- Increase Engagement & Comprehension
- Design Effective Lessons

■ SCHOLASTIC

Dedication:

To America's newest teachers

Series Editor: Lois Bridges

Development Editor: Dana Truby

Designer: Maria Lilja

Copyeditor: David Klein

Cover photo: Bruce Forrester

Interior photos: Noah Berger/AP and Jim Burke (where noted)

ISBN 13: 978-0-439-93454-1

ISBN 10: 0-439-93454-0

Contents

Introduction

"You don't teach a class. You teach a student."
—Paul Baker, *Integration of Abilities*

Many of us still think of *memorable* teachers from
our childhoods, those great ones we remember
throughout much of our adults lives with a sense
of reverence for all they gave us. Such teachers have three
characteristics: they are competent in their subject matter,
care deeply about students and their success, and take on a
distinctive role in the classroom. Though we all aspire to
be memorable teachers, it is *effective* teachers that we must
strive to become and which our students need us to be.
We cannot say we have taught something if our students
cannot, with some independence and fluency, show us they
learned it by using or doing what we taught them.

The ten elements of effective instruction in this book
are divided into three sections: Instruction That Works,
Classroom Culture, and Curriculum Basics. Each of the ten
elements, drawn from extensive reading and research, as well
as my own daily experience as a classroom teacher, focuses
on guiding principles of effective teaching. Here are the "big
ideas" of teaching that will help you promote understanding
(not just recall), engage students in meaningful inquiry, and
develop students' ability to master such work in the future.

Before examining what effective teachers do, let's highlight some key findings from the National Research Council (NRC) on how people *learn*. In 2000, the NRC identified three key findings:

1. Students come to the classroom with preconceptions about how the world works. If their initial understanding is not engaged, they may fail to grasp the new concepts and information being taught, or they may learn these concepts in order to pass a test, but revert to their preconceived ideas outside the classroom.

2. To develop competence in an area of inquiry, students must: (a) have a deep foundation of factual knowledge, (b) understand facts and ideas in the context of a conceptual framework, and (c) organize knowledge in ways that facilitate retrieval and application.

3. A "metacognitive" approach to instruction can help students learn to take control of their own learning by defining learning goals and monitoring their progress in achieving them. (Brownsford, Brown, & Cooking 2000).

Keeping in mind that teaching is a skill that can be *learned*, let us move on, giving ourselves permission to try, even to fail, knowing that these are necessary stages if we are to join the ranks of those effective, even memorable teachers who inspired us to join this profession in the first place.

Effective Instruction Self-Assessment

For each of the items below, record your answer between 1 and 5.

1 Never   **2** Rarely   **3** Sometimes   **4** Usually   **5** Always

Effective Instruction

☐ I vary my instructional methods and use a range of teaching strategies.

☐ I teach my students how to think and learn.

☐ I assess students' understanding and use the results to improve my instruction.

☐ I incorporate a variety of tools and technology to enhance my instruction.

Classroom Culture

☐ I support all students to ensure their success.

☐ I maintain a safe and productive learning environment in my classroom.

Curriculum Basics

☐ I teach skills and knowledge in context and through application.

☐ I organize all instruction around meaningful conversations and sustained inquiries.

☐ I make connections to the students' lives, other studies, and the world.

☐ I design lessons and units for maximum learning, understanding, and engagement.

After completing this self-assessment, identify those areas of most urgent need. Then go to the corresponding chapter and learn what you can do to improve in that area.

Instruction That Works

1. Vary Your Instructional Methods and Strategies

Kids need variety to stay engaged in their learning. They need to know that if they can't learn the lesson one way, you will use another approach to help them understand whatever you are teaching. It helps to consider learning like a house that you want your students, by one means or another, to enter, inhabit, and eventually own. It makes sense, of course, to bring them in by the most obvious route: the front door. Yet, that is sometimes locked, and so students need to know that there are other ways of getting in, what Gardner (1999) calls alternate "entry points," which allow them to use what they know to learn what they do not—yet. This level of commitment to students' success pays great dividends in the classroom. You'll see greater engagement from your students and, just possibly, a deeper belief in their own efficacy. Your students will come to realize that you and your class are there to help them do what many believed they could not. That's why it's important to "differentiate" your instructional content, process, or products according to students' needs (Tomlinson 1999).

Guiding Principles

1. Provide multiple entry points into every subject or lesson.

2. Employ a range of instructional modes.

3. Use a variety of group formats and configurations.

4. Describe and demonstrate each strategy or technique.

5. Develop students' background knowledge using different techniques.

Provide multiple entry points into every subject or lesson.

Every student who comes into your class has personal interests, experiences, and abilities that he or she can use to succeed in school and life. Yet kids often do not know their own strengths and needs; nor do they know how to use them to learn. Here are a few approaches you can use to help students connect with what you teach:

Analogies: Make comparisons. Daily life in the Civil War was like... (Social Studies)

Stories: Tell a story about a certain experience, focusing on the choices you had to make along the way. (Health)

Numerical representations: Have your students examine what happened during the Depression by graphing data. (Economics)

Visual explanations: Challenge your class to imagine the characters in *Othello* are on a football team and then describe the role of each character. (English)

Dramatic interpretations: Have students role-play a Supreme Court case based on a constitutional amendment you are studying. (Government)

Essential questions: Ask the big questions, such as "Why do living creatures have to die?" (Biology)

Hands-on or manipulative techniques: Have students design and build a city or structure using the shapes and concepts we have studied lately.

Consider beginning your class with these activities. Upon entering the classroom, students would see the essential question and begin writing a response to it. Once students have grasped the question, you can go on to design students' learning experiences in ways that challenge them to:

Make inductions, deductions, and inferences, and draw conclusions: Have your class review Lincoln's major decisions and draw conclusions about what kind of leader he was, providing specific evidence to support your analysis. (Social Studies)

Organize information by various principles: Through discussion, generate stages of moral development, then have students arrange and apply them to the characters in a novel. (English)

Repeat a sequence of progressively more difficult tasks: Give students leveled math problems, perhaps bronze, silver, gold, so they can see their growing mastery. (Math)

Navigate their way through a carefully designed messy experience that requires them to troubleshoot increasingly difficult problems: Challenge students. Design an ecosystem, adding new complications in addition to those that naturally occur; require students to monitor and evaluate data as the experiment unfolds.

Such experiences require some initial understanding or mastery of the content. You should increase the challenges only when the students show they are ready for the next level of work.

Keep in Mind Your English language learners (ELLs) rely on you to provide multiple ways into academic content that is unfamiliar or beyond their capacity to understand. Ask yourself (and your students) what other means you can use that will help ELLs navigate the material in your class.

Employ a range of instructional modes.

Entry points are the openings through which your students can gain access to what they need to learn. Instructional modes, on the other hand, are the techniques you choose to guide their learning so that the hard work that real understanding requires can take place. How should you choose which instructional mode to use? Begin with the question, "How can I design a learning experience that will lead my students to a full understanding of what I want them to learn?" Think of modes as similar to tools: The right tool for the right job gets you where you want to go (and where your students need to be). Consider these methods or instructional approaches when you are deciding how to help students "uncover" the material, which is to say understand, be able to use, and remember what they learn.

11 Instructional Strategies to Use (Besides Lecturing)	
Instructional Approach	**How It Works**
Demonstrate	Show students what a successful performance looks like.
Read to Think	Read excerpts or short texts aloud as a means of introducing a subject or getting students to think about it from different perspectives.
Write to Learn	Have students write formally or informally to discover what they know about a subject, or to synthesize their learning.
Investigation	Design an inquiry for your students in the library, classroom, or computer lab that asks them to find and make sense of information.
Simulation	Provide a range of roles students can play in reader's theater, mock trial, etc.

Construct	Provide materials and ask students to design and create an original project—a model, a project, or a poem.
Discussion	Create a structured, purposeful discussion of the material in different configurations—pairs, trios, or large groups.
Reciprocal Teaching	Ask students to teach what they have learned to others in a group or the class as a whole.
Problem-Solving	Place students in the middle of a problem they must solve using their understanding of the material.
Generate	Require students to be generative thinkers who come up with their own questions and problems, answers and solutions.
Reflect	Ask students to reflect on their learning process to increase their understanding of what they learned as well as how they learned it.

Tech Note! Use technology in ways that require kids to inquire, investigate, or create. Tech approaches can be productive so long as you choose them with the end in mind and not merely as electronic worksheets.

Use a variety of group formats and configurations.

Because people are naturally social, it makes sense to use this characteristic to help them learn. Studies consistently find groups, if used effectively, are one of the most powerful instructional strategies for improving comprehension and increasing engagement. Collaborative learning also proves ideal for English language learners who need frequent opportunities to practice their spoken language and hear how others use it. Research consistently shows that specific grouping strategies, such as literature circles (Freeman and Freeman 2007) and reciprocal teaching (Palincsar and Brown 1984), are effective with heterogeneous learners in different subject areas. The idea of learning together is not new, of course: People have always gathered in circles to solve the problems they face, realizing, as the sayings go, that "two heads are better than one," and "many hands make light work." As Margaret Wheatly wrote, "Human beings have always sat in circles and councils to do their best thinking, and to develop strong and trusting relationships" (2002). Here are some guidelines for using groups to enhance instruction in your class:

Provide structure and establish a clear outcome for each group, holding students accountable as both a group and individuals. In English, for example, a teacher could use small groups to have students generate a list of words that describe a character, then vote on the one that *best* describes the character; and find evidence from the text, that backs up this one "best" word.

Arrange groups heterogeneously unless students have common needs or problems that can be more efficiently addressed through targeted group instruction (e.g., ELLs needing a quick tutorial on a specific topic). In my room, for example, I will ask students to form groups based on whatever ensures the right combination for a given task (e.g., "Everyone form groups of four made up of no more than two boys, and the group must include two people from the opposite side of the room.")

Evaluate students' group work and have them reflect on their own processes to identify what they do well and what they could improve on as a group and as participants in that group. Ask them, for example, to list what they contributed to the work and to evaluate its effect on the final result. Post your group evaluation questions in the classroom to help students keep them in mind.

Avoid overusing groups by carefully considering whether the task would be more effective if done individually. In a math class, for instance, students can benefit from working together to solve complex problems, but they also need to work independently for the concepts to take hold. You should always have a clear instructional rationale for groups, even if it is, "It's Friday afternoon—working in groups will energize them."

Use both formal and informal grouping techniques for *different purposes* that allow students to work with different classmates. Some days I say, "Turn to a neighbor and compare your interpretation with theirs," but on other occasions, when students are reading different stories, for example, I might have them meet with those reading the same story to discuss a specific question.

This last point merits more discussion. Both group formats, formal and informal, serve the common goal of providing powerful learning experiences, but there are some important differences:

Informal Groups: Such groups can be pairs or small groups of three or four, but are temporary, usually formed by students who sit next to or around the student for the sake of a quick conversation about a problem, a text, or an idea. Informal groups serve to generate ideas and solutions, clarify thinking, respond to others' work, or compare interpretations and processes. Finally, they are well suited as a way to follow up on individual work or a class discussion since they provide a context for students to elaborate on the ideas that arose in full-class discussion or while doing an assignment individually.

Formal Groups: While informal groups might work together for anywhere from one minute to a full period, formal groups are more structured, with each person having a specific role, such as the discussion director in a literature circle, for example. These groups are more assignment-based, existing for the length of a project, a sustained inquiry or experiment, or the time it takes to read a book as part of a literature circle. Also, there is a clearly defined outcome for which people are accountable as both individuals and a group; this sense of "we must hang together or we will all hang separately" is important in such groups.

Tech Note! Online forums such as blogs and threaded discussions offer powerful new ways to use or extend classroom groups. Creating one of these virtual forums can be of great benefit to ELLs, shy students, or those who need more time to formulate their responses during group discussions.

Two other aspects of grouping deserve clarification. Research consistently shows that when teachers use groups, group size and group selection make a critical difference. The following table provides an overview of the different types of groups and their uses:

Use this Grouping	If You Want...	Have students...
Pairs (2)	informal, quick conversations where students can compare solutions,	turn to a neighbor and confer.
Small (3–4)	deeper discussion from several perspectives,	work with their assigned mixed-level group.
Large (5–7)	more student participation than full-class discussion allows,	blend assigned groups or count off to create quick groupings.
Full Class	to debrief with the whole class about what they discussed in groups or to survey the whole class's response to material.	participate from their seats.

Ability grouping is only appropriate and effective when students share an instructional need; grouping low-performing students with low-performing students leads to even lower performance. More importantly, mixed-ability groups consistently show the greatest instructional gains. Useful ways to arrange groups heterogeneously include sorting kids by birth month, personal interests, assigned numbers, number of siblings, favorite animal, or alphabet.

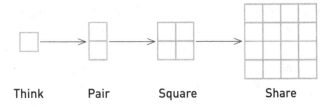

Think   Pair   Square   Share

One of the most effective techniques for using informal groups is commonly referred to as think-pair-square-share. Students begin by working individually, solving the problem, responding to the text, and making their initial hypotheses. Once they finish this step, they pair up and discuss their work, comparing solutions and ideas, then borrowing new ideas from each other as they arise. Next, the pair "squares up" with another pair to expand and elaborate on the discussion before returning to a full-class discussion facilitated by the teacher, who can then address enduring questions and gaps in students' understanding before moving to the next phase of the lesson. A history teacher, for example, might assign individual students different constitutional amendments to read and interpret, then ask them to generate an example to illustrate the amendment's principle. After that, they pair with others who studied similar amendments and discuss as a pair, until finally the whole class engages in a discussion of constitutional law and how it works.

New Teacher Note While groups are an important and powerful strategy, they are only as effective as their implementation. If allowed to choose their own groups all the time, kids will, of course, gravitate to their friends, which often undermines the social and academic benefits of working with others. Be clear and consistent in assigning groups and ensuring that students stay and work in those assigned groups.

Describe and demonstrate each strategy or technique.

Students come to school to learn what they don't already know. The better they understand what we expect them to do—how to play a certain role in a group, how to conduct an experiment, how to use a tool—the more likely they are to succeed. As the Chinese proverb says, "Tell me and I'll forget; show me and I may remember; involve me and I'll understand." To prepare them for their "involvement," we must model what to do so they will know what to do when asked to do it themselves. When working with new techniques or strategies, or asking students to apply those they already know at a higher level, you may need to describe and demonstrate before, during, and after.

Before using the strategies, students need to know what an effective performance looks like.

During, you need to clarify and refine students' application of the technique.

After they finish, it is often beneficial, even necessary, to have students reflect on their use of the technique or strategy to help them improve their application next time.

For example, I will begin by modeling for students how to use it, then follow up by having them reflect on how they used the graphic organizer and how it helped (or didn't help) them. Through modeling, we demystify for students those tasks that they may think are beyond them because they do not know how to break them into steps. As the following suggestions show, language plays a crucial role in such effective instruction. When describing or demonstrating, consider the following:

Use "warm language" to help students understand and engage with the content. To "bring students inside," you must be explicit and complete in your descriptions and demonstrations, raising powerfully worded questions and extending invitations (as opposed to issuing orders). "Cool language" serves to remind and summarize; warm language invites and stimulates interest and confidence. (Bain 2004)

Demonstrate the language you want them to use when writing or speaking by using it yourself; extend this support by using sentence starters for different thought processes so that students learn to use this language in context.

Sentence Starters to Kick-Start Student Thinking

Cognitive Strategy	Sentence Starter
Goal Setting	"My purpose is..." "My top priority is..."
Tapping Prior Knowledge	"I already know that..."
Visualizing	"If this were a movie..."
Making Connections	"This reminds me of..."
Summarizing	"In a nutshell, this says that..."
Adopting an Alignment	"I can relate to this author because..."
Clarifying	"To understand better, I need to know more about..."
Revising Meaning	"At first I thought ___, but now I..."
Reflecting and Relating	"A conclusion I'm drawing is..."
Evaluating	"I like/don't like ___, because..."

Provide clear, sequential explanations of what to do and how to do it, reinforcing the teaching, if necessary, by providing a handout or listing these steps on the board. When first offering such explanations, avoid specialized vocabulary that might confuse or intimidate. Instead, use more familiar, informal language. In a lab, for instance, you might begin by emphasizing the importance of following the proper sequence of steps in a particular procedure; in addition, you might give them a sheet with numbered steps they can check off as they complete each step. As the experiment unfolds, you could introduce specialized vocabulary for them to use when describing what they observe.

Introduce big concepts and basic principles through stories or analogies to illustrate and provoke connec-tions; as students show initial understanding, add details and complexity; when they are ready, replace the familiar language or analogies with more specific and complex terms and concepts you want them to understand and use. In a health class, for example, a teacher could begin a unit on addiction by asking students how video games or cell phones are similar to a drug. Then, as the class moves into the unit, the teacher introduces more specialized vocabulary related to addiction.

Use visual devices—overheads, whiteboards, chalkboards, Smartboards, LCDs—to explain and demonstrate, serving as a visual reference for the processes and solutions your class generates throughout the discussion.

> **Keep in Mind** English language learners are most successful when teachers have high expectations and do not deny access to challenging content and when teachers explicitly teach and model the academic skills and the thinking, learning, reading, writing, and studying strategies all students need to know. (Olson and Land 2007)

Develop students' background knowledge using different techniques.

Background knowledge, especially about academic subjects, is essential to success in school. Background knowledge includes subject-specific knowledge about procedures and processes, as well as facts and related vocabulary; it also includes relevant knowledge of historical events, mythology, the Bible—what E. D. Hirsch (2006) has termed "cultural literacy." Deep background knowledge is strongly correlated with adult success, according to Marzano (2004). Background knowledge means what a person already knows about a subject. While a student might feel sure that the knowledge is accurate, it might be outright incorrect, based on belief instead of evidence. Effective teachers understand that a student's background knowledge is a part of him or her. It connects to the student's self-image and self-esteem. Developing students' background knowledge always involves determining what they think they know about a subject and creating a learning experience that will help them affirm or revise what they know in light of new experiences. At the same time, it requires providing a safe and supportive environment in which they can say what they think they know and revise their thinking in public without fear of humiliation. Marzano (2006) identifies two aspects of background knowledge: the student's ability to process—understand and remember—such knowledge, and the type and quality of such information as it relates to the academic context in which the student must use it. Some argue that such processing is fixed, genetically determined, but Marzano notes studies that show cognitive processing can be improved through such techniques as cognitively guided instruction. You can enhance your students' background knowledge and their ability to access and use that knowledge by doing the following:

Assess what students already know about the subject you are studying by having them write about and discuss it with others to raise initial questions the teaching can help answer. In a science class, for example, you could begin by asking students to explain what evolution is and how it works, providing examples to illustrate what they mean.

Provide direct instruction in a way that will prepare your students to understand and remember the bigger ideas you want them to learn. This is especially important when it comes to academic vocabulary students need in order to understand a text or complete an assignment. When teaching about tone in relation to a poem, I demonstrate the meaning of several words and show how to use them.

Use indirect means to develop such background knowledge by having students read articles or textbooks, watch videos, investigate a subject on the Internet, or interview people who may have important knowledge about that subject. Students studying the Holocaust, for example, can go to the National Holocaust Museum Web site, where they can view and read stories of survivors, as well as see photographs of those who survived.

Jim Burke

Incorporate the relevant background knowledge into multiple lessons, through multiple means; increasing the frequency of exposure and the amount of information improves understanding and recall of the information. When introducing key terms and ideas, first discuss, then post the terms to the wall for reference.

Provide activities to enrich the background knowledge: field trips, guest speakers, performances, programs like Facing History, or ACCESS (Burke 2005). When teaching health, for example, invite a speaker from a local health food store or a culinary academy to speak about food.

It may seem obvious, but one aspect of background knowledge that deserves attention and emphasis is your own knowledge about and passion for the subject you teach. The more you know about any subject, the more you have to draw on to help your students understand and remember it. If you have a deep understanding of some aspect of geometry or physics, for example, and kids in your class have deep knowledge of a sport like baseball, you can take advantage of your fluency to connect your subject to your students' areas of expertise and thus help them better understand the material. Famed physicist Richard Feynman was renowned for his use of stories and analogies to help students understand concepts that first eluded them, drawing on the students' background knowledge in one area to help them understand and remember new, unfamiliar material. More important, I suspect, was the evident joy he found in *doing* and in learning about his field, which is something we should all convey to our students, not just through a lesson but by drawing upon all that we continue to learn. Walt Saito, a legendary math teacher at my school, was famous for telling his students about the math problems he created for himself over the weekends, or while traveling to school on the train. As one student told a researcher studying my class, "It's weird, but Mr. Burke tells us all about what he reads all the time. He actually talks about books and all that stuff like it really matters and that makes us think it's more important."

2. Teach Students How to Think, Learn, and Remember

While learning is natural to all of us, academic learning often is not. We think of such learning in the context of a "discipline" or we say students must develop the discipline needed to think, learn, and remember information, ideas, and processes specific to our different content areas. Certain habits of mind come into play in all school subjects; however, each one demands that students develop what Gardner (1999) calls a "disciplined mind." Such thinking requires guidance, which is where you come in. You make the decisions about where to begin, which problems or texts to try first. Through such scaffolding and guidance, you develop students' independence and cultivate the habits of mind necessary to grapple with progressively complex material. This kind of instruction demands a solid understanding of the brain and how it works—the chemical-emotional basis of learning and memory that makes those synapses fire and connect as they work to understand and, later, to recall. Metaphors abound when it comes to thinking about these cognitive processes, but the words that recur most frequently in my investigation all evoke the idea of intellectually wrestling with the content, during which the learner comes to know the deep meaning and structure of the material. As you will read in other chapters, learning is also a social process; thus, it is ideal to have students work in robust ways, "grappling" with and struggling to understand data, texts, or problems. Finally, it is perhaps useful to think of the mind as the gardener does the soil, asking yourself what you can do as the teacher to help students learn to prepare and maintain their own soil, allowing them to grow and harvest their own learning, according to their own style and strengths.

Guiding Principles

1. Be methodical and strategic when teaching students to learn, think, and remember.

2. Cultivate different types and aspects of intelligence in all students.

3. Instill key habits of mind in students to help them succeed in school and life.

4. Initiate students into the thinking specific to your subject matter and discipline.

Be methodical and strategic when teaching students to learn, think, and remember.

How we learn, think, and remember is as familiar and visible to us as the operating software running in the background of our computers. That is, we don't worry about it so long as it works. Sadly however, like that software, we often find ourselves at the limits of our capacity to process and store information, and we have no choice but to "upgrade" our system. So it is with our cognitive processes: They are fine until we start encountering more difficult material, at which

point we need to understand the limits of our thinking so we can improve our capacity to understand and remember these complex ideas. Thus, our students should encounter new and more difficult ideas, texts, and problems each day as they burrow deeper into the material. The question is, can thinking, learning, and memory be *taught*? Can intelligence and memory be enhanced, expanded?

Jim Burke

Cultivate different types and aspects of intelligence in all students.

Einstein avoided words and numbers, finding in images and "thought experiments" (i.e., visual problems, such as what would happen while riding a light beam alongside a train) a way to understand and express his insights about the universe. Effective teachers help their students, even those who are not Einsteins, identify and develop their individual talents; they also help them acquire or improve upon those talents they lack. Such effective teachers make room for students to explore their gifts in order for them to better understand the potential and processes of their own mind. Many recent books emphasize the importance of developing "different minds" (Gardner 2006; Pink 2006) and ways of thinking (Sternberg 1997), which Kelley (2005) calls "faces of innovation." Kelley quotes a claim published in *The Economist*, that "innovation is now recognized as the single most important ingredient in any modern economy." Thus, you will be most effective when you make use of students' different capacities, for then your instruction meets not only the needs of the individual student but the society as a whole. In this sense, effective instruction is grounded in both the personal and the public worlds. Reflecting the complex demands of these different worlds, Kelley identifies ten "personas," which he divides into three categories—learning personas, organizing personas, and building personas. Each is a way of thinking or working that students need to explore. We should create regular opportunities to incorporate these personas into our curriculum. While each persona draws on and develops different skills, Pink (2006) argues that strong teachers can and should address them all through an integrated, dynamic curriculum.

Here are Kelley's personas, followed by my summary of his ideas, as they would apply to education:

LEARNING PERSONAS

Jim Burke

The Anthropologist: Functions as an observer, developing insights into people, cultures, and environments, which he or she uses to solve problems. In health class, for example, students might create and conduct a survey about the time they spend online or on cell phones, and then use that data to show that excessive use has academic, personal, and health costs.

The Experimenter: Learns through trial and error, taking calculated risks, and creating a series of prototypes; these yield information the experimenter uses to create new solutions. In an environmental biology class, for example, teachers might ask students to study global warming by creating a model of what will happen under different scenarios (e.g., as it grows progressively hotter) and how such conditions will affect a specific ecosystem.

The Cross-Pollinator: Ranges across subjects, fields, and domains, then translates what is learned into actions and solutions. The teacher might ask students to use ideas from one field (e.g., evolution [biology], the free hand [economics], a certain mathematical principle) to explain something in another field. A student in my English class, for example, used a very complex mathematical equation to isolate and explain how the plot and themes interacted with each other in a novel.

ORGANIZING PERSONAS

The Hurdler: Relishes overcoming obstacles and solving problems encountered during the learning process, often bending the rules to come up with innovative solutions. One might, for example, appoint such a person to head a group project in which you expect various obstacles to arise.

The Collaborator: Brings people together and leads from within the group, helping others use their talents to solve a common problem that leads to success for all. When using literature circles, for example, you might appoint a student to the role of discussion director.

The Director: Gathers people and works with them in ways that inspire new thinking and creativity. This is often a key role for you to play as you move around and consult with individuals or groups, using your knowledge to challenge them to go deeper or be more creative on a particular assignment.

Jim Burke

BUILDING PERSONAS

The Experience Architect: Loves to design experiences that do more than just convey information; creates experiences that change, inspire, and move people to achieve specific outcomes. In a health class, for example, such students would thrive if given the chance to create an ad campaign on subjects like drugs, healthy eating, relationships, or racism.

The Set Designer: Responds to the challenge of creating a stage, transforming a space into an environment that achieves a particular effect on an intended audience. In English or history class, where students might reenact events from history or portions of stories, such students respond to the opportunity to create props and sets.

The Caregiver: Anticipates and addresses the needs of customers and coworkers; motivated to provide for the emotional and physical well-being of others to ensure the success of an individual or a group. In many academic classes, such students appreciate the opportunity to work with others who might need additional help. Ask this kind of student to work with a couple of ELLs or perhaps a student you know who has reading difficulties.

The Storyteller: Maintains morale and develops understanding by telling compelling stories to inspire others or communicate specific values or ideas. Provide such a student with the option to create a compelling story—in writing or using different media—as part of a study of World War II, teen health, or environmental biology.

While each persona draws on and develops different skills, Pink (2006) argues that strong teachers can and should address them all through an integrated, dynamic curriculum.

Instill key habits of mind in students to help them succeed in school and life.

Effective teachers, like great coaches, shape their students' abilities and processes into habits, achieving a level of fluency that fosters higher-level performances. Such "habits of mind" are essential to academic and adult success, but can only be inculcated through instruction that affords rich opportunities to learn and apply them, as well as receive the feedback needed to refine those habits. Key habits of mind you should teach your students include to:

Gather and evaluate information from multiple sources and senses. In a history class, for example, students could gather and evaluate information from different sources, including blogs and Web sites, on issues such as immigration, then use what they learn to support arguments in presentations, papers, or discussions.

Respond critically to what they read, view, hear, and experience. In an American history class, for example, students could examine the rhetorical devices used in World War II propaganda posters to persuade citizens to save gas or buy bonds.

Take responsibility for their own learning, including how they work with others, seek help when they need it, and advocate for what they need in order to succeed.

Experiment with new ideas and perspectives. In English, for example, you can have students write about the same subject from different perspectives to inspire new thinking and refine their original arguments on a subject.

Use their knowledge of themselves and the world to learn and remember. A physics teacher might use, for example, a student's interest in skateboarding to help him understand certain principles.

Be flexible in their thinking and processes. Students often want to fix on an interpretation of a literary text. To teach them more flexible but no less responsible reading, ask them to find evidence for other interpretations of the same text.

Reflect on their thinking and processes in order to better understand how their minds work when trying to do, learn, or remember something. This might mean asking students to answer such questions as, "What questions did I ask to arrive at that final result?" or "What techniques did I use and how did they lead to this result?"

Here are some other, more general suggestions for getting students to be more generative and reflective thinkers, while at the same time teaching these skills and developing these abilities:

Ask students to provide a variety of alternative explanations, interpretations, or solutions, and to explain the strengths and weaknesses of each, using evidence to support their thinking.

Provide students time to "mess around" with ideas, materials, or processes and to think about not just what they came up with, but how they did so.

Create fun but educational constraints within which students must work to solve problems or create, thus forcing them to be flexible and "think outside the box."

Require students to explain why certain readings, interpretations, solutions, or results are invalid or incorrect as opposed to always focusing on the right answer (a variation is to focus on what students do *not* understand instead of what they do).

Generate questions students can use to approach, solve, or explain a text or problem.

Initiate students into the thinking specific to your subject matter and discipline.

Each subject comes with its own language, both formal and informal. To discuss poems, novels, or essays with any precision, students need literary and rhetorical terms. So it is with all subject areas now, for between the language of the discipline and the precise terms reflected in state standards, students must learn how to read, use, and understand the disciplinary discourses of science, humanities, social sciences, mathematics, health, and other

subject areas. It is not just the language, however, that students must learn; they must also work and think as scientists, writers, historians, and mathematicians in these respective fields.

Effective teachers initiate students into the language and ways of thinking specific to a given discipline by:

Modeling how practitioners within their subject area speak, work, and think, as they go about "doing" science, history, or writing.

Providing students lists of discipline-specific words or sentence starters (on handouts, the board, or posters) they can use to explain a procedure, discuss an author's tone, or advance an argument based on the Constitution.

Bringing in examples of how professionals function in a given field by showing video footage of the scientist thinking, a sequence of rough drafts that illustrate the writer's composing process, or reading about the steps the individual followed to arrive at a solution; you can also invite such people to speak in your class.

Teaching students directly, in context, the academic vocabulary needed to do the work and understand what they read in a subject area.

3. Assess Understanding and Use the Results to Improve Your Teaching

Long before video cameras existed, my tennis coach used an 8mm camera to assess my game. Unlike today's cameras, it did not offer immediate feedback; we had to wait a week for the film to be processed, then we had to find a projector, a screen, and a dark room in which to view the film. Nevertheless, it offered both of us relevant, useful feedback for improving my game. In contrast, winning or losing a match was like a report card: if I won, it was an A; if I lost, an F, but the result was not educative. The camera, that visual feedback of my performance, however, transformed a loss or a win into a lesson that my coach could use to adjust his instruction and show me what he meant when he said, "You're dropping your wrist on your backhand shots." My backhand immediately improved once I could finally see what he had been saying for so long. Today, of course, using a video camera to capture and analyze a performance is just standard procedure; back then it was a revelation. The same approach should be taken with assessment in the classroom, with the teacher adapting instruction based on feedback *during* the process of teaching a clearly defined idea or process that is important to the learner.

Assessment is not to be confused with grading. Students typically look only at the grade, ignoring any comments they don't consider useful to improving their performance. Nor should assessment necessarily be equated with testing, though tests are clearly one means of assessing what students know and can do. Effective instruction uses assessment to clarify what should be taught, to determine how much progress your students have made, and to show you how you can use this information to inform and improve instruction. In short, assessment should be used to help both student and teacher learn. It should be purposeful, not punitive; consistent instead of confusing; not mundane, but meaningful; and aligned with the content standards, as opposed to the teacher's personal passions.

Guiding Principles

1. Assess students *before* teaching, to determine their current knowledge and skill levels.

2. Use multiple means and measures to assess students' performance.

3. Define the objectives and criteria clearly before you begin to teach the lesson or unit.

4. Teach students to assess their own progress through goal-setting and reflection.

5. Provide useful, specific, meaningful feedback throughout the learning cycle.

Assess students *before* teaching, to determine their current knowledge and skill levels.

Effective instruction begins where students *are* and develops in them the knowledge and skills they need to get where they *need to be*. Some students enter your class with a wide range of personal and academic experiences which prepare some of them to do the work you will ask of them, while others will have no prior exposure to the topic or task. Teaching students who are unaware of what they already know is both inefficient and ineffective. It is inefficient for several reasons. First, you may waste time on material they already know when you could be building upon that foundation. Second, your students may know nothing about the subject, so your initial instruction will have to be repeated when you circle back to teach them the necessary information or skills you assumed they already had. Such assessments do not need to take a long time; most can, in fact, be conducted informally, through a variety of quick measures that give you a sense of where to begin and how to adapt your instruction in light of your academic goals for students. You can determine your students' needs before they begin by:

Giving them a pretest you create or purchase from a commercial publisher. At the beginning of the year, for example, you could give students a test based on their state standards; such tests are commonly provided by commercial publishers now.

Observing them working on an assignment that gives you some sense of their initial level of understanding or ability. In my Advanced Placement Literature class, for example, I give students a difficult poem the first week and watch them work through it on their own and in groups to evaluate how they work and think.

Using a graphic organizer, such as the KWL, which asks students to explain what they know, want to know, and what they learned by the end of the assignment. Thus, a social studies teacher might begin a unit on the Depression by using a KWL organizer to find out what students know.

Looking at informal writing, such as notebooks, responses, and drafts that offer insights into next steps; you can also have then fill out an "exit card" on which they explain their understanding of the material and give the card to you as they leave. In a science class, for example, students might write down three bullets summarizing key ideas from that day's lesson or a lab they worked on.

Preparing a class discussion with the primary purpose of determining what students know about a certain subject; for example, give them cards they can hold up to indicate their understanding (yes/no, green/red) at specific junctures in the lesson. In health, for instance, you might survey students about their knowledge of sleep and sleep-related behavior.

Keep in Mind ELLs often enter the class with a wide range of school experiences and levels of academic knowledge, depending on their previous access to formal schooling. Obviously, ELLs who had access to school in their home country face a different set of challenges from those of the ELLs who have never attended school. Prior to beginning a new unit or assignment, take time to find out whether your students have academic skills such as taking notes, outlining, researching—or whatever skills might be necessary for the unit you are about to begin. Also, consider what specialized academic vocabulary they must know to do the required work.

Use multiple means and measures to assess students' performance.

Assessment seems to come down to several complex but useful questions:

- What are the means by which we can best determine the extent of a student's knowledge and skill in a specific area?

- Given the constraints of time within which we always work, which of the possible assessments is the most appropriate for this situation?

- And, finally, what are we willing to accept as evidence that a student has learned what we taught?

As a teacher, you know some days are better than others; thus, you know how unfair it would be to have an administrator suddenly show up to evaluate your performance on a bad day and, based on that single observation, assess your effectiveness as a teacher. Effective assessment, therefore, requires that we use different means to measure what students know and can do before, during, and after we teach them. Improve your teaching by using these three different assessments to meet the current needs of your students in light of the content standards you are teaching:

Diagnostic Done *before* you begin to actively teach, these assessments help you create a learning profile of each student by giving you information on what he or she knows and can do. Such information is essential in helping you determine what content to teach first, what methods are most appropriate, and how you should organize the instructional sequence. Diagnostic assessments are not graded; that is, students might get a low score but the score is not entered as a grade that would punish students for what they do not yet know. In my AP English class, for example, I give students a test on literary terms to see how much they know at the beginning of the year.

Formative Used *during* the instructional sequence, formative assessment is an ongoing measure of students' progress toward specific learning goals. Such measures give specific information about individual student performance, which you can use to adjust your instruction; the information on such assessments also provides useful information to the students for improving their performance. Formative assessments can be both formal (quizzes and exams) and informal (observations, discussions, journals, interviews, having one student restate another's ideas). Such assessments may be graded, but can also be used simply as feedback without being graded. When deciding what kind of assessment to use, consider the context and what would most promote learning. History teachers might, for example, use one or more of these formative measures to assess students' understanding of key ideas about the Civil War.

Summative Used *after* the instructional unit is over, summative assessments evaluate the extent to which the student learned the material you taught. These typically culminate in some performance or product that measures understanding and mastery of the content standards. Formal measures include a major exam (e.g., multiple choice, short answer, essay), a project, or a performance that provides an authentic assessment of what students learned. Summative assessments are graded, ideally using

Jim Burke

criteria established up front, so students knew what they were expected to learn and how they would have to show that learning. In an environmental science class, for example, students could take a traditional exam or they could give a detailed multimedia presentation showing all they had learned during the unit on hurricanes.

It's easy to get overwhelmed by all you are expected to accomplish, yet assessment is only useful if it is effective. As you know from students' performance on many state-mandated tests, motivation is a key factor in both learning and assessment. McTighe and O'Connor (2005) write that, "students are more likely to put forth the required effort when there is:

Task clarity: When they clearly understand the learning goal and know how teachers will evaluate their learning

Relevance: When they think the learning goals and assessments are meaningful and worth learning

Potential for success: When they believe they can successfully learn and meet the evaluative expectations."

> **Keep in Mind** Some students may find it hard to express themselves verbally or in writing and may need alternative ways to show what they have learned. ELLs, for example, may not yet have the language to do what you have asked but, if given the chance to show what they have learned by some other means, will be more likely to succeed. Whenever possible, offer alternative assessments or options, such as the opportunity to show understanding orally or through visual media, which allow students to be measured according to their strengths.

Define the objectives and criteria clearly before you begin to teach the lesson or unit.

We all need a map to guide us and a destination in mind to give us some means by which to make decisions, to evaluate the importance of different information. For teachers this means their state's content standards; yet it also means those other lessons, ideas, and skills we want our students to learn along the way. By defining the objectives and criteria for your students, you define them for yourself and thereby take the crucial step that leads to more effective instruction. Without such an instructional compass, we feel like Yogi Berra who warned, "If you don't know where you are going you will end up somewhere else." Assessment, if used to improve instruction, asks you to begin with the end in mind, so your instructional sequence—the materials, methods, and measures—will lead to that result. Yet students cannot easily work toward an end they cannot understand or see; for this reason, it is essential to clarify for them what successful performance on assignments looks like. By defining the instructional objectives and the criteria by which those results will be evaluated, you give them, and yourself, a useful means by which to evaluate the importance of different information and thus prepare for a successful performance at the unit's conclusion. The primary source for these objectives is, of course, your state standards or, in the case of Advanced Placement classes, the College Board; effective instruction aligns itself with the

content standards appropriate to your class. You can define these objectives and establish the criteria by:

Using the assignment sheet to identify the specific learning objectives they should master by the end of the unit or lesson. At the top of the handout for students' summer reading essay, for example, I list the specific goals of the assignment so that they know what I am looking for and what matters most.

Posting the objectives in clear, student-friendly language on the board to keep in mind what it is you are trying to accomplish. A biology teacher might, for instance, list the goal of identifying the parts of a cell as part of students' lab that day.

Demonstrating for students what a successful performance looks like, so that they will know what they are trying to learn to do. A shop teacher might, for example, demonstrate how to use a certain technique when using a power tool so that students see how to do it and what the final result looks like.

Providing examples that you or previous students created, so that students see what the final result looks like. If possible, show several different examples, so that students can understand what distinguishes an excellent performance from one that is merely proficient from one that is unsuccessful. I often make copies of essays and other writing assignments to use as exemplars in my class, then put them on the overhead and verbally annotate them.

Giving students the scoring rubric or criteria that will be used to evaluate their performance before you begin the unit or lesson so they know what is expected of them. A history teacher might give students such a rubric for an upcoming debate.

New Teacher Note! Ask your colleagues for examples of student work or samples of the different assessments they use; these give you something to respond to when creating your own.

Teach students to assess their own progress through goal-setting and reflection.

It falls to us to evaluate the quality and progress of our own work, as it does to other adults in their fields. Such self-assessment is common among those who are driven to improve their performance. Athletes crave information, using scores, times, and other relevant data to refine their performance. Businesses and salespeople constantly seek and use information to improve their methods, markets, and products. Such information can then be used—*must* be used in many fields and professions—to set goals that will lead to even better results. One cannot achieve these results, however, without the opportunity to reflect on the data in light of the methods used. In the end, what we realize, and what we must help students realize, is that individuals are responsible for their own success whether they are salespeople, athletes, law enforcement officers, students, or teachers. You can teach students to assess themselves by:

Asking them to set personal goals at different points throughout a unit or lesson—before, during, and after—related to the larger objectives you spelled out at the beginning. Such goals should be personal and specific, as well as measurable. An English teacher might, for example, ask students to set a goal of using no passive verbs in a piece of writing as part of a larger unit of effective writing.

Pausing at appropriate opportunities to assess progress toward their own goals, specific benchmarks, or those objectives you established at the beginning. Such self-assessments can be done in journals, on worksheets, or index cards, which might then be turned in to you so you might monitor their progress as well as their ability to evaluate their own work. Students in a chemistry class, for example, might write up an interim report to present to the class on their results so far, and the possible implications of these results.

Using a rubric to evaluate students' progress toward these established criteria; in addition, you might consider having them reflect on which strategies or methods have been more or least effective in helping them reach these objectives. In an economics class, for example, in which students must compare two theories, students might examine the devices and strategies they used to create an effective comparison. Rubrics, however, can be overused, preventing students from receiving more specific, responsive feedback. And sometimes they are just not effective.

Creating time for students to reflect on the choices, actions, or strategies that led to that result. Such metacognitive reflection about their process, products, or performance can be done by writing or discussing with others what they did, how they did it, and why they did it that way. Also, ask students to use more than one process, then evaluate which one was best and why, in light of the results. In a math class, for example, have students reflect on the process by which they solved a particular problem, focusing not only on the decisions they made, but the alternative ways they could have solved it.

Having students compare their work on this assignment with that of similar but earlier work to gain a clearer measure of their progress in this particular area of their learning. Students in an English class, for example, might look at earlier drafts of a particular paper or papers to see how they have progressed as writers.

Provide useful, specific, meaningful feedback throughout the learning cycle.

Feedback received after a performance can be useful for future assignments, but if it cannot be used to improve performance on the current assignment, it loses its value. For a student who struggles to solve a problem in mathematics, for instance, effective feedback provides the student with insight into how to solve not just the problem at hand, but that type of problem in general. So it is with problems, performances, and processes in all subject areas. Moreover, the feedback, if it is to make a difference, should come throughout the process. Think about how video games and other simulations offer immediate and precise feedback about what the player did right or wrong; such information allows a player to improve by avoiding a mistake or repeating a certain action in the future. Feedback comes in a variety of forms: written, spoken, or visual. Of course, it takes time to give such information to students; all the more difficult if you have short periods or large classes. Still, few efforts make a bigger difference than providing such feedback. You can provide students useful feedback on their performance by:

Monitoring work in class on an assignment and noting those areas in which students are doing well and where they need guidance. Once you have gathered the performance information, have students stop working, so you can provide feedback, including specific examples gleaned from class that day. In a science class, for example, take time to make observations about how students are using the instruments and conducting their experiments, pointing out particular actions that are good or should be avoided.

Collecting their work in the middle of the process— such as, a rough draft of a paper that will be revised— and giving specific feedback to each student on a few key areas, or skimming through all the papers to find those key areas of trouble common to them all, then providing feedback the next day in class through direct instruction, using examples and details from their papers. In my English classes, for example, I will skim through a set of papers to evaluate how effectively the writing is organized, then copy a few examples and use those both to set the standard and guide my instruction the following day, giving students specific techniques they can use to improve their own papers.

Designing discussion questions that reveal to both teacher and students the current level of understanding.

Using evidence, such as individual evaluations or group work, or a performance video to show them those areas that are strong and weak, making time to meet and discuss with them ways to improve in those areas. In a public speaking class, for example, a teacher might videotape individual performances, then meet with students to deconstruct their performances. Based on these conferences, students can make refinements and receive additional feedback on subsequent performances.

Tech Note! Use programs such as PowerPoint to create quick quiz questions to project during a lesson or discussion. Students can indicate their answers by raising their hands or indicating the correct answer (a, b, c, d) to each practice multiple-choice question.

4. Use the Right Tools and Technology to Enhance Instruction

Students in my colleague's class resisted the research paper she assigned them, but when she created an anonymous MySpace account—one with a fake name, no identifying personal information, no school affiliation—three sophomores found her within 24 hours and wrote to invite her to be on their "Friend list." Kids typically run when we say, "Write!" but routinely write on their cell phones and computers with vim, vigor, and a wide variety of colorful language. They often turn in work that lacks attention to detail and organization but will spend entire weekends sorting and organizing their photographs on MySpace. Many boys who resent school assignments lose themselves in games like *World of Warcraft*, where they invest hours, even days, learning a dizzying array of strategies, "cheats," and rules needed to win.

Arguing the merits of today's video games, Stephen Johnson (2005) writes:

> The great secret of today's video games that has been lost in the moral panic over *Grand Theft Auto* is how difficult the games have become. That difficulty is not merely a question of hand-eye coordination; most of today's games force kids to learn complex rule systems, master challenging new interfaces, follow dozens of shifting variables in real time and prioritize between multiple objectives.

In short, precisely the sorts of skills that they're going to need in the digital workplace of tomorrow.

In the classroom, you have an increasingly wide range of tools, certainly more than the filmstrip and chalkboard of my youth. In this chapter we look at what tools you have and how you can use them to improve your instruction.

Guiding Principles

1. Use an array of tools and technologies to enhance your teaching.

2. Choose the tools or technology most appropriate to the instructional situation.

3. Make the most effective use of tools and technology in the classroom that you can.

4. Challenge students to think critically and creatively using tools and technology.

5. Provide an appropriate environment for using such tools and technology.

Use an array of tools and technologies to enhance your teaching.

Something is a tool if you use it to accomplish a specific purpose; thus it is not entirely right to suggest that tools and technology are distinct, for the truth is that we use technological solutions

Jim Burke

as tools to help us complete a wide range of tasks. Tools come in all forms and serve many different functions, depending on the context in which they are used. We use tools to present, analyze, capture, collect, organize, communicate, investigate, create, collaborate, learn, and remember. Use the following list to find the tools and technology that will improve your instruction and best facilitate students' learning:

To present
- LCD projector (for laptop or DVD/VCR)
- Presentation software (e.g., PowerPoint)
- Overhead projector
- MP3 player (for audio)
- Interactive whiteboard
- Podcast
- Whiteboard/Chalkboard
- Web site
- Television monitor (with DVD/VCR)

To organize
- Index cards
- Sticky notes
- File folders, labels
- Graphic organizers
- Software (database or spreadsheet programs)
- Color-coded materials, markers, or pencils

To collect, measure, capture, or record
- Camera (video or digital)
- Graphic organizers
- Recorder (audio, MP3, digital)
- Software (spreadsheet and database programs)
- Instruments (such as, lab instruments like probes)
- Handheld devices

To analyze
- Software (spreadsheet programs)
- Graphic organizers
- Calculator (financial, scientific, graphic)
- Instruments (scientific)

To generate
- Poster paper
- Sticky notes
- Whiteboard/chalkboard
- Graphic organizers
- Software (brainstorming programs such as Inspiration and Visual Thesaurus)

To communicate, collaborate, or investigate
- Online information sites
- E-mail
- Blogs and threaded discussions
- WebQuests
- Simulations

Jim Burke

Choose the tools or technology most appropriate to the instructional situation.

Even as I write this, I can see my father telling my ten-year-old self not to use the wrench as a hammer—for the umpteenth time. When it comes to instructional tools and technology, choosing the right tool for the job is still of great importance. When I was a kid, schools had nothing expensive to break. No one had any interest in playing with a filmstrip projector. Now we have machines in our rooms worth thousands of dollars (if we are lucky) which, if broken, will probably take a long time to get replaced. And because we have so little time to spare, we strive to choose the most effective instructional tools. Too often, though, we fall prey to the allure of using a computer to do in 20 minutes what could be done in five on paper. Or we use the overhead for work that should be done on the whiteboard, where it can be left and reviewed later on. To help you decide which tool to use, ask yourself these questions:

- What problem does this tool or technology solve?

- Can this task be completed just as easily with a paper and pencil? I often have students create a "paper PowerPoint" by drawing a slide and crunching the information down to a header and three main bullet points, then present or discuss it with a group or the class.

- What features can you use (e.g., color, formatting, spatial arrangement of information) that can improve instruction and understanding? In English, for example, when teaching writing, I often use different colors when teaching aspects of writing or grammar.

- What skills and knowledge do students need in order to be able to use this tool or technology? And, do you have the necessary time to provide this instruction *and* still have them use the tool for the primary task? In math, for example, graphic calculators are increasingly common, but require some training.

- What handouts or other complementary materials can you provide students to help them further process and understand what they are learning? A history teacher might, for example, give students a graphic organizer as a means of considering a subject from different sides.

Tech Note! It is easy, especially in schools with resources, to assume that all kids have access to computers and other tools you want them to use. Equity and access are important guiding principles when using technology. If you require students to participate in online discussions, for example, be sure they have access through school in case they do not at home.

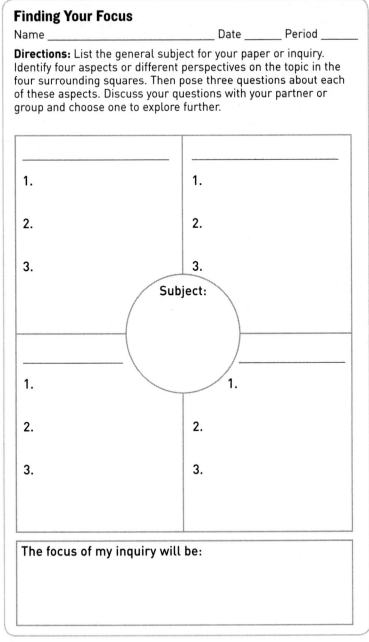

Finding Your Focus

Name _____ Date _____ Period _____

Directions: List the general subject for your paper or inquiry. Identify four aspects or different perspectives on the topic in the four surrounding squares. Then pose three questions about each of these aspects. Discuss your questions with your partner or group and choose one to explore further.

_____   _____

1.   1.

2.   2.

3.   3.

Subject:

_____   _____

1.   1.

2.   2.

3.   3.

The focus of my inquiry will be:

Make the most effective use of tools and technology in the classroom that you can.

In the early years of computers, many teachers used computers as electronic worksheets, having students sit before the screen doing what they could have done easily, and for much less money, on paper. No doubt this still goes on, but we have learned much more about how to use technology to enhance instruction and learning. For example, in their study of mathematics instruction in the United States, Germany, and Japan, Stigler and Hiebert (1999) examined teachers' use of visual aids to help students learn mathematics. They focused in detail on the difference between using the board vs. the overhead, contrasting the American teachers' commitment to the overhead to the Japanese teachers' structured use of the board:

> Whether they use overhead projectors or chalkboards, [American teachers] use these visual aids to keep students' attention directed toward the information of the moment.... Many preservice teacher-training programs offer advice on using overhead projectors in just this way... [being] told to cover up all the items on the transparency except the one being presented, then to move the cover down to the next item, and so on.... Japanese teachers use visual aids for a very different purpose: to provide a record of the problems and solution methods and principles that are discussed during the lesson. The first item of information in the lesson is placed at the far left of the chalkboard; the next item, whether presented by student or the teacher, is written next to it; and so on. The record builds, left to right, as the lesson proceeds. Many Japanese teachers finish the lesson with a full chalkboard, showing a complete record of the lesson.

Perhaps the central lesson implied by this example is that in order to learn, students need to be able to revisit information during the learning process, that learning broken into episodes or fragments fails to deepen our understanding or remain in our memory. Consider these suggestions to make sure you use technology and tools in ways that make a lasting instructional difference:

Provide feedback and follow through on the work students do when using tools and technology, treating

the WebQuest or graphic organizer as the beginning, not the end of the assignment. I typically have them synthesize the contents of the organizer into a paragraph, which creates a useful opportunity for further writing instruction.

Give students clear instructions in the proper use of the tools and technology. This may mean copying the tool to a transparency or presenting on an LCD to model how to use it.

Plan ahead when using technology to make sure everything is ready to maximize instructional time. I always go by the computer lab ahead of time to make sure the printer is working and stocked with paper, for example.

Avoid using features (e.g., sound, graphics, fonts, animation) that distract from the material you want students to learn.

Choose the tool or technology that yields the greatest learning result while also developing additional knowledge and skills. For example, having students use spreadsheet software also teaches them to analyze and organize data, as well as use computers and new software programs.

Challenge students to think critically and creatively using tools and technology.

Regardless of whether we choose paper or Web pages, screens or boards, the question is always: How does this specific tool allow you to add capacity and complexity to your instruction that not only helps students understand but extends their understanding? One year, for example, I wanted to bring a wider range of texts into my class, freeing us from the limits of black-and-white on paper. Looking to the Internet for inspiration, I came up with the idea of a "digital textbook" (Burke 2001) I called *The Weekly Reader*. (www.englishcompanion.com/room82/weeklyreader.html). Thanks to the computer, I could create a table of contents for this digital textbook, which included video, images, audio, color, simulations, and more, all of which my students could easily access, experience, and write about in a short weekly paper. My goal, aside from giving them the chance to explore the bigger textual world, was to extend their work by asking them to read new and more demanding texts; thus, they took a traditional literacy  (reading) to the next level and, in the context, learned new ways to think about and make sense of what they read, hear, and see. To incorporate such complexity and critical thinking into your curriculum, you can:

Ask yourself what more you can add to each assignment that would increase the challenge and complexity in useful, educational ways. For example, a teacher could have students take digital photographs of their lab results, then annotate the images before presenting them to the class using an LCD projector.

Use technology to show the same subject from multiple perspectives. For example, an English teacher could show a sample paragraph on an LCD projector in regular black letters, formatted as a traditional paragraph, followed by the same paragraph in different colors, to show, for example, the supporting details. Finally, that same paragraph might be parsed into lines to show more visually how the writing is organized.

Make room for students to invent and explore possibilities you may not anticipate or know about. Once a student asked me if his group could transform a group project they were doing into a "paper Web site" to take advantage of the different design elements inherent in Web sites.

Ask kids to reflect on the tools or technology they are using, and results they are getting. For example, while students are preparing a PowerPoint presentation, you can ask them to stop and examine the organizational pattern and content of the slides and how that will achieve the intended effect.

Discuss the different ways students used the tools, the questions they asked, and the strategies they used to get their results; also, compare these results with others, making the process part of the instruction so that others see how else they might obtain similar or even better results in the future. In a science class, for example, students can discuss how they used various instruments and applications to yield, gather, and manage data.

Provide an appropriate environment for using such tools and technology.

All the tools and technology in the world will make no instructional difference if you cannot provide the necessary conditions to use them and learn. Many teachers take students into the computer lab, prepared to use an entire period for online research or other work on the computers, only to find different operating systems on machines, no paper in the printer, an empty toner cartridge, missing software needed for the assignment, no mouse on three machines and no working keyboard on two others. Or the Internet is down that day. Follow these simple but useful suggestions to make sure you have a successful class when using tools or technology:

- Prepare ahead of time to be sure you have all necessary materials, equipment, or resources and that they are appropriate, working, and available.

- Estimate how much time students will need in the lab, library, or shop; also, figure out how much time the whole assignment will take and evaluate the benefit of that expenditure of time.

- Consider what support materials (e.g., handouts) or additional tools (e.g., graphic organizers) would help students succeed on this assignment. I often write out specific instructions, sometimes providing a screen shot of what students should see when, for example, they first participate in an online threaded discussion.

- Design assignments that make maximum use of students' attention and energy, and the school's resources. For example, students can complete a WebQuest in pairs, or do a lab in teams.

- Have examples of similar work on hand for students to refer to as they work, so they know what a successful performance of the task looks like. On my Weekly Reader Web site, for example, I post sample papers and the rubric I use to evaluate the writing on that assignment.

Classroom Culture

5. Support All Students to Ensure Success

If you begin by assuming your students can meet your high expectations, it transforms the relationship and your role, making you a guide, a mentor charged with helping your apprentices learn what you are there to teach. Still, no one method will reach all the kids in your class, which is why the new "three Rs"—rigor, relevance, and relationships—are so important. That first R, rigor, sets the bar you will help them clear. The other two Rs represent the support you will provide, support based on your commitment to meaningful learning (relevance) and to the students themselves (relationships). The following guiding principles offer a useful framework to consider before, during, and after you teach a lesson or unit.

Guiding Principles

1. Identify and teach to students' strengths.

2. Provide different types of support throughout the learning experience.

3. Differentiate instruction whenever possible.

4. Use different methods, strategies, and configurations.

5. Demonstrate and restate your faith in your students throughout the instructional process.

Identify and teach to students' strengths.

Whether you describe them as "affinities" (Moran, Kornhaber, Gardner 2006), "minds" (Levine 2006), "intelligences" (Gardner 2006), or "cognitive strengths" (Sternberg 2006), each student comes into your class knowing many things. The catch, of course, is that those things may not fall into the area you teach. In his research into cognitive strengths, Sternberg found that there were three primary types: analytical, creative, and practical. In a number of different studies, he found that students working within the domain of their primary strength not only learned more, but were more engaged and did measurably better on multiple-choice tests that stressed memory over deep understanding. Summing up his findings, Sternberg wrote: "When we teach and assess in ways that respect different strengths, students learn and perform better." Here are some suggestions to help you teach to your students' strengths:

Identify your students' strengths early through a questionnaire, informal assessment, or any other means that will reveal this information. Return to these periodically, asking students to reflect on these strengths, how they help, and how they have been using these strengths to learn and remember. During the first week, I deliberately provide opportunities to show what they can do as readers, writers, speakers, workers, and test takers.

Monitor student work—on paper, in discussions, during labs—to find strengths; point these out to students, referring to them and drawing on them in the future. During a lab, a science teacher may notice a student's consistent effort to focus and guide the group, using certain helpful questions.

Let your students use their strengths in order to learn or show what they know. Students with strong verbal abilities might be asked to write a summary of a certain mathematical principle, or allow students with artistic abilities to first draw what they will later explain in writing.

Jim Burke

Organize students into groups based on strengths, inviting them to learn and demonstrate their mastery of the material by means of their strength. Sternberg organized students by cognitive strengths—analytical, creative, and practical—and had them read the same psychology textbook, but allowed each group to work with it according to their specific strengths. Students excelled, with each group demonstrating equivalent gains on the traditional, multiple-choice tests.

Encourage and allow students to use what they know in another area—their culture, sports, or other academic areas—to learn what you are teaching them in your discipline. In English, for example, I have had great success when asking students to visually represent the action in a Shakespeare play by allowing football players to use the visual language of football plays to describe what the characters in the story are doing. By using a visual language, they understand how to explain what they thought they could not. I help them get back in the academic game.

Provide different types of support throughout the learning experience.

Support comes in many different forms; here are some useful suggestions:

Physical—Students with physical limitations may need help in doing certain tasks that require coordination, strength, or stamina they do not have.

Material—Keep extra supplies on hand, and be mindful, when assigning work that requires equipment (e.g., a computer, graphic calculator), that not all students have access at home.

Cognitive—Many thought processes, such as those involved in reading and writing, require specialized thinking that is not intuitive to most students; providing cognitive sentence starters helps them learn the necessary language structures and allows them to complete the task.

Emotional—Students have many pressures they are coping with; monitor students' emotional condition and show compassion by listening, asking, encouraging, and praising, to help them through difficult times.

Procedural—Write directions on the board and handouts in clear, easy-to-follow steps; go over these, providing examples, if necessary. In a lab or shop, take time to demonstrate any new procedures or how to use new instruments and tools.

Cultural—Evaluate students' knowledge of a given subject necessary to complete another task (e.g., biblical literacy necessary to understand a literary work); based on evaluation, provide the necessary background knowledge on the event, person, era, or idea.

Social—Teach students the skills needed to work with others, especially if they have no prior experience of working with others in such a way. This includes teaching students the language needed to participate in class discussions.

Academic—Students need guidance in taking notes, taking tests, reading and writing about academic subjects, and using academic conventions. Provide lists of sentence starters or specialized terms they should use, and explain when, how, and why to use them, offering examples when appropriate.

Linguistic—ELLs need help understanding the language; provide this support by assigning your ELLs a native speaker nearby to explain; also, check to make sure they understand as the learning experience unfolds.

Background Knowledge—While related to the cultural literacy mentioned on the previous page, background knowledge also refers to knowledge of ideas, processes, events, and other subjects that prepare students to complete some assigned task.

Keep in Mind Echevarria and Graves (2003) identify the following key considerations for working with ELLs with language and learning difficulties: "provide abundant guided practice for acquisition of concepts; adjust the pace of instruction according to students' needs; allow extra time to complete assignments; praise students' efforts and use positive reinforcement; partner students with others sensitive to their learning needs; provide alternative activities when a task may draw undue attention to students' disabilities...; plan and use appropriate behavior management techniques; employ learning strategies known to be effective with students with disabilities."

Differentiate instruction whenever possible.

Differentiating instruction does not mean creating 35 separate lesson plans for the 35 students in your class. Tomlinson (1999) describes it as "a teacher's response to [a] learner's needs guided by general principles of differentiation such as respectful tasks, flexible grouping, and ongoing assessment and adjustment." Nor does it mean lowering your expectations to ensure some diminished, empty form of success. Instead, differentiation aims to address the needs of students at all levels, including your highest-achieving students, who need to be challenged in ways the others are not necessarily prepared for yet. Tomlinson argues that teachers can differentiate three areas of the curriculum—content, process, and product—according to each student's readiness, interests, and learning profile. As discussed before, such a profile might be based on Gardner's "intelligences," Sternberg's "cognitive strengths," or Levine's "minds." The following suggestions offer a range of instructional solutions for differentiating instruction in your class:

Use a group configuration, such as a lab team, which allows each student to assume a different role, some of which make greater cognitive demands than others.

Provide a range of problems, texts, or projects to choose from, each one representing different levels of difficulty, but all of them based on the same subject or text you are trying to teach. In a social studies class, the teacher might allow students to choose from an article in *Time*, a local paper, or a primary source document on World War II, each one more difficult than the other.

Assign support materials, such as word lists or graphic organizers, which students can use at different levels of ability. In English classes, for example, discussing and analyzing characters can be difficult, so provide students with a list of character words to choose from. (See examples above.)

Character Words

aggressive	frantic
aloof	gregarious
anxious	intelligent
bitter	irritable
bored	loquacious
carefree	manipulative
conceited	naïve
conniving	nervous
curious	outgoing
deceitful	picky
demure	scrupulous
devoted	sincere
easygoing	testy
envious	unpredictable
	welcoming
	worried

Give students a variety of topics to choose from when writing, some of which make greater demands and allow for a greater range of responses than others. In a health class, for example, writing topics could range from summarizing, to comparing and contrasting, to analyzing the cause and effect of different drugs.

Prepare additional prompts, questions, or problems for students who finish early or need additional support or challenge. The teacher could post these on a side board, keep on the class computer, or store on index cards.

Allow alternative routes for students with special needs, such as audiobooks, to complete a reading assignment in your class.

Keep in Mind As students move into the higher grades, the demands of school typically play to girls' strengths (verbal and linguistic), providing fewer opportunities for boys to use their dominant abilities (spatial) in hands-on ways. Look for ways to let students choose the method that plays to their individual strengths, and ask yourself if this content, process, or product creates an obstacle to the success of any members of your class.

Use different methods, strategies, and configurations.

Mel Levine (2006) identifies eight distinct neurodevelopmental constructs that represent individual students' strengths: attention, temporal-sequential ordering, spatial ordering, memory, language, neuromotor functions, social cognition, and higher-order cognition. Some tasks or assignments demand that students use more of these functions than others, a fact that has significant implications when you are making instructional choices. Levine says of writing that it "is the largest orchestra a kid's mind has to conduct," which explains why some students have so much difficulty with all or certain aspects of the writing process. The following list offers suggestions for how to meet students' needs using a variety of approaches and configurations:

Provide regular opportunities to collaborate, in various group configurations, on assignments to allow students to help and learn from each other. Nystrand (2006) found no other instructional approach showed greater gains in comprehension, engagement, and memory than structured, intentional use of discussion in small- to medium-sized groups.

Employ a range of instructional modes: reading, writing, speaking, visually representing, and physically enacting or constructing. In a history class, for example, students might read primary source documents and articles from South Africa, which they then adapt into speeches, which they rehearse and present—in character—as part of a forum on, for example, apartheid.

Allow students to choose which strategies they will use on certain tasks once they have learned to use them independently through direct and guided instruction and subsequent practice. Science teachers can teach students to take a variety of note-taking formats, but eventually students should be free to choose the one that best aligns with their learning style.

Give students a variety of ways to demonstrate their understanding, whenever appropriate. While you should not accept a video in lieu of a research paper when you are focusing on writing instruction, the documentary is a valid alternative in many other situations. Though you want them to read challenging literature, consider when it is acceptable to allow students to listen to audiobooks instead as an alternative, and how you might have them respond to or take notes on such a reading experience.

Demonstrate and restate your faith in your students throughout the instructional process.

Throughout this process of learning, students are figuring out whether to see themselves as someone who can do what school—and the world—asks them to do, or someone who cannot. Students who work with a teacher whose words and actions, whose tone and attitude, convey confidence and faith, will be more likely to weather the storms of doubt inherent in the process of learning. You can convey this sense of confidence and assurance to students by doing the following:

Use positive, optimistic language when speaking to both the class and individual students, assuring them that you would never ask them to do something you were not sure they could do—or learn to do. When introducing a writing assignment, for example, I typically explain how important this is for their success in school and life, then, whenever possible, sit down and write with them.

Show faith in students by giving them room to choose or asking them what they think about a topic, text, or problem. When possible and appropriate, I will give students the option of coming up with their own alternate topic, though they must first clear it with me to make sure it meets the same instructional objectives.

Maintain high expectations, but convey your commitment to helping them satisfy those expectations through your attitude, language, and actions. I consistently remind them that I have high expectations, but am willing to meet with them before or after school to help them meet these expectations. I also pepper my language in class with remarks such as, "Yes, this is a demanding assignment, the most demanding so far, but I know you are ready for it and I'm willing to help you every step of the way."

Communicate your enthusiasm for their ability and progress through comments—spoken and written—in and outside of class, to the students themselves, as well as to their parents and the class in general, finding specific but genuine qualities. Some schools have online student systems like Power School or School Loop, which is what I use to send out praise notes or notes of encouragement, which take only seconds to write.

Keep in Mind Leave your personal biases and prejudices—about race, ethnicity, gender, certain groups, or issues—at home. Enter the classroom with the belief that all students *can* learn and *can* succeed if you provide them with the necessary emotional and cognitive support.

6. Maintain a Safe, Productive Learning Environment

Creating a safe, supportive environment does not mean protecting students from any possibility of failure; nor does it mean lowering your expectations until they are doing the academic equivalent of playing tennis without a net. Rather, it means establishing a culture of purpose and rigor seasoned with laughter and learning, a culture of high expectations served on a bed of genuine support designed to help kids meet those high expectations, a culture that celebrates that success once it is achieved. When expectations are high, however, pressure can get to the best of us; so to increase the likelihood of achieving such bold objectives, you must create the necessary conditions and sense of emotional security that your students require in order to accomplish what they did not think they could.

Guiding Principles

1. Establish and maintain high expectations for quality of work and behavior.

2. Create clear policies regarding behavior and enforce them consistently.

3. Cultivate a safe, respectful environment at all times.

4. Consider students' developmental needs.

5. Celebrate students' success in and out of the classroom.

Establish and maintain high expectations for quality of work and behavior.

Studies consistently find that high expectations are an essential ingredient to success in school and life. Such demands create a sense of urgency, a feeling of importance to the work at hand; and, if spelled out in the syllabus in a tone that implies faith, · students will respond in kind, placing their faith in you to help them meet your challenging standards. It is one thing to say, "Jump over that ten-foot bar!" and quite another to teach them how to do it. And kids today are under so much pressure in all areas of their lives that they need all the help you can offer. A recent survey by kidshealth.org found that kids between the ages of 9 and 13 worried most about grades, appearance, problems at home, being liked/fitting in at school, and being out of shape or overweight. Many of these concerns clearly relate to students' self-esteem, and nothing improves self-esteem more than real, measurable success. Thus, from the day students walk into your class, they should find a closely linked and clearly conveyed combination of high expectations and the support needed to achieve that end. To create such a culture of high expectations, try the following:

Connect all instruction to the world at large. Explain the real-world importance of what you teach. In my English classes, for example, I consistently emphasize stories like the one about the local fire department that narrowed the applicant pool by first giving a writing test (which they asked our English department to help them evaluate).

Provide examples of what a successful performance looks like by displaying these samples on the overhead, bulletin board, or handouts so students get a sense of the level of your expectations. Rubrics can further clarify your expectations by defining what they must do to achieve the desired result. A social studies teacher, for example, could put on the overhead and analyze aloud a sample essay from a previous exam to better prepare students for the next one.

Spend more time on assignments, helping students dig deeper for the big ideas instead of equating high expectations with work piled high. Overwhelming students with busywork frustrates and alienates them, creating hurdles that only the most ambitious are willing to jump. Math teachers at my school, for example, found that students were more likely to do their homework and do it well if they had five instead of ten problems to do.

Use a grading system that allows students to take risks and learn without fear of punishment. In the ABC-I grading system, anything below a C is considered incomplete and must be revised or redone. This shows that some need more time and guidance, but that everyone can meet your standards if they make the effort and get the necessary help.

Validate students' struggles. It's important to acknowledge that it *is* hard. In my class, for example, I often acknowledge what I found difficult about a particular text and then talk about how I solved the problems I encountered, discussing the specific strategies I employed.

Create clear policies regarding behavior and enforce them consistently.

A safe environment is predictable, unlike the environment that many of your students go home to each day. This does not mean that you should do the same thing every day in the same way, like some "edubot"; rather, it means that you are consistent in how you structure the class, and how you handle situations and treat students. Such a classroom culture is the consequence of policies (some of which may be developed *with* students) designed to hold students accountable for their behavior, while also being flexible and responsive to individual students' needs. These policies, spelled out at the beginning and revisited throughout the school year, exist to help your students learn and succeed. In the absence of such policies, students withdraw in order to protect themselves. Follow these suggestions when creating and enforcing policies in your class:

Define all policies about behavior and student work in clear, student-friendly language. See, for example, my sample User's Guide to Mr. Burke's classroom, on the next page.

Communicate these policies in writing (syllabus, handout, bulletin board), speech (refer to, reiterate, and clarify them), and through your own actions, which should always demonstrate the principles that govern your class.

Enforce policies completely (e.g., don't apply only those parts you want to) and consistently (e.g., to all students in all situations); to do less would undermine your own credibility and the effectiveness of the policies themselves.

Clarify and reinforce how these policies relate to students' success. In a first period class, for example, emphasize that you do important work at the bell for those opening minutes and that late = missed learning = lower grade in your class.

Apply these policies in a sensitive way, avoiding whenever possible any gesture that would embarrass or otherwise humiliate a student. Instead of saying sarcastically to a frequently late student, "Well, Mr. Murphy, so glad you could join us," talk to the student in private after class, stressing the importance of being there on time and clarifying your policies.

Mr. Burke's Class: A User's Guide

If...	Then...
You need to go the restroom,	Please ask for a pass, which is required at all times in the hall.
You ask to go the restroom regularly,	I will recommend you go before class and ask you to wait until class is over.
You have an electronic device out where I can see it,	I will assign detention as required by the school electronic devices policy.
You bring food or drink into the classroom,	I will ask you to either store it or dispose of it.
You have special needs of any kind (difficulty seeing the board or reading my handwriting, are disturbed by noise, etc.),	Please let me know ASAP so I can accommodate you if at all possible.
You wish to speak to me about a grade you received,	Please write a note and attach it to the assignment stating your concern with the grade.
You wish to meet with me to discuss an assignment, a problem or anything else,	Sign up on the calendar and let me know so that I can be there and ready to help.
You do not have a computer at home,	You are welcome to use mine before school and during lunch period.
If you cannot afford or find any resources I encourage or require you to buy,	Let me know so that I can help you.

Cultivate a safe, respectful environment at all times.

Nothing is more difficult—or more important—in a learning environment than for a student to say, "I don't understand," or "Could you explain that again?" Such phrases, which roll off the tongue of confident, experienced learners with ease, even pride, are prized moments in the life of the emerging student, the one who asks now because he really wants to know—and thinks he can understand if told again, in slightly different language. However, such moments are full of danger, vulnerability: If someone were to laugh or otherwise embarrass the student at such a moment, that student might never raise her hand again. I once had a student who did not speak in class until the second semester. In response to a simple yes/no question, Simone raised her hand slowly—the whole class was looking at her, thinking *but not saying* "Wow, Simone has her hand up!"—and said only, "No." Because we had worked so hard to create a climate of safety in the classroom, and because we respected what a huge step it was for Simone to do this, we all knew that we must not say anything or we would frighten her away from ever speaking again.

Such respect is all the more important these days given the cultural, political, and personal perspectives and experiences students—and teachers—bring into the classroom, many of which can

be incendiary given the nature of those tensions. Because of these issues and the problems that can arise, your classroom needs to be a shelter from that storm, a place where everyone comes in and feels safe to speak and be listened to by their peers. Without that security, that respect, that trust, real learning is impossible. Here are some ways to cultivate such an atmosphere of security and respect:

Model the use of respectful language at all times when speaking to or about students—or your colleagues—in and outside of class. For example, if your colleagues in another department teach writing in a way you don't agree with, you should say only, "I realize that other teachers have different expectations appropriate to their subject area, but in this class we write this way for the following reasons...."

Establish your policies and values immediately related to respect in the class, discussing why you value these and how such traits will serve students in the increasingly global and diverse world. In most classes, for example, it is appropriate to collaborate, which, we should emphasize, is essential to their success in the adult world, where collaboration with different people, who may even be in a different country (online collaboration) is common practice. In my class, I typically say, "It's essential that you learn to work with others as this is a necessary skill for success in today's workplace, where the person you work with might live in India and work with you via a video screen on your computer."

Create the conditions for taking risks by giving students language they can use if they do not know how to discuss a subject or by framing the activity with phrases such as, "Now, this is difficult for many people, so when we talk about it, I want us to respect each person when they take their turn. That means no laughing if someone were to make a mistake or otherwise embarrassing them."

Speak with students privately about how they handled a situation or used language, making them aware, but not uncomfortable. If appropriate, discuss with them some other ways they could have said or handled something that may have caused some offense or tension. I will typically ask a student to stay after or come back at recess so I can point out what was said or done, and asking them "Can you think of another way to handle that situation or respond to that person that would show more respect?" I might then suggest a few others.

Evaluate your own materials for language or content that might upset or offend students; this also means evaluating your curriculum for the treatment or absence of women, people of color, and other groups. If such content is an inevitable part of the curriculum, consider how best to address it and make it part of the curriculum. When I started teaching a senior class, for example, the books were all written by white authors, only one of whom was a woman. Little by little, for we never have enough money to do things in bold moves, I introduced new authors and different, more inclusive topics.

Consider students' developmental needs.

Students do not all develop in the same way on the same schedule; nor is there one generic idea we can call "development." Darling-Hammond and Baratz-Snowden (2005) suggest that crucial areas of development include social, cognitive, physical, emotional, and linguistic, all of which play an essential role in academic and adult success. In a chapter titled "Preparing the Brain for School," Eric Jensen (2005) distinguishes between the different grades, characterizing the brain of the 5- to 12-year-old as one of "wonder, ready to take on new challenges including reading, writing, arithmetic, and the world of reason." Summarizing others' findings, Jensen indicates two periods of major brain development during this first phase: around 6 or 7, and again around 11–12. During these stages, the brain shows new cognitive capacities for increasingly abstract thinking as well as a greater understanding of the world beyond the child. Toward the end of this first stage—that is, as students enter middle school—they show an increased awareness of social networks and make often baffling decisions about who they spend their time with, how they act, and what they eat, all of which can interfere with their performance in school. The high school years, during which hormones are in full swing, bring additional physical changes that further complicate the emotional and cognitive changes already underway. All this development suggests a brain rich in potential but characterized by inefficiency. As if the developmental picture were not complex enough, Jensen (2005) says, "Although most brains become physically mature between ages 18 and 30, it takes boys until about age 24 to catch up to girls' brain development." Darling-Hammond and Baratz-Snowden (2005) identify four areas teachers should understand if they are to be effective:

- The constructive *nature of knowing*—the fact that we all actively attempt to interpret our world based on our existing skills, knowledge, and developmental levels. This means that teachers need to understand what students already know and believe, and be able to build bridges between students' prior experience and new knowledge. This includes anticipating student misunderstandings in particular areas so that they can be addressed.

- *Cognitive processing*—how people respond to, perceive, and process information, retain it in short- and long-term memory, and retrieve it. This includes the importance of organizing information so that it can be connected to other ideas, incorporated into a schema for learning new information, and retrieved when needed.

- *Metacognition*—how people learn to monitor and regulate their own learning and thinking. This includes knowing how to teach students to think about what they understand, what they need to learn, and what strategies they can use to acquire the information they need.

- *Motivation*—what encourages students to become and remain engaged with their learning. This includes knowing what kinds of tasks, supports, and feedback encourage students to put forth effort and strive to improve.

You have so much to teach, so little time in which to teach it; yet if you don't consider how the minds of your students work, if you ignore those other aspects of their development, they may leave class without having learned what you wanted them to know. Or, they may learn it but not remember it unless you help them connect what they learn today to all the other nodes in the growing branches of knowledge in their brain. Here are some general suggestions for teaching in the midst of students' developmental evolution:

Provide concise directions broken down into steps, going through each one individually; also, do not muddle your message by inserting digressions, sarcastic remarks, or critical comments that would cause emotional reactions. On writing assignments, for example, whether the directions appear on the board or a handout, list the steps sequentially.

Teach like a doctor, not a judge: Continually assess and monitor what students need, how they are responding; then make instructional choices based on your diagnosis instead of criticizing them and thereby eliciting counterproductive emotional responses and undermining their confidence and motivation. Writing is tough for most students, and you'll always find errors. Consider the difference between saying, "I was appalled by the errors in your writing. Terrible! I wondered if you had any idea how to write at all!" and "I noticed on the papers certain patterns of error which we will look at in the coming weeks. Today I thought we would look at just a few examples and discuss how you can avoid these problems in the future."

Make room for mistakes during the learning process. The absence of punishment gives students the room they need to experiment, to figure out how they can best solve the problem or understand the material. When teaching writing, for example, I often have students write several different versions of an introduction, encouraging them to take risks and stressing that they will not be punished with lower grades for doing so.

Create outlets for physical energy. They already have it and if not used, it will interfere with learning. In grades 4 to 9, for example, allow students to act out texts and historical events or construct models by way of understanding concepts or solving problems.

Select tasks with students' developmental needs in mind, providing contexts to explore those aspects of their own development or issues in their own lives through young adult literature or online investigations. In health classes, for instance, subjects like brain development, sleep, and relationships offer meaningful subjects that students are motivated to understand.

Celebrate students' success in and outside of the classroom.

For all the talk about standards and high expectations, about holding kids accountable and pushing them to prepare for the demands of the world to come, there is little talk about the importance of joy and love of learning. The philosopher Simone Weil, reflecting on the purpose of education, wrote, "The joy of learning is as indispensable in study as breathing is in running." And Albert Einstein, who made many poignant remarks about education, argued that, "love is a much better teacher than duty." When we think about celebration, we must also think about whether what we celebrate has any real meaning and value to the people involved. Is getting a high score on a standardized test an event of genuine value to students? If it is a test like the ACT or SAT, the success is meaningful because it has real results, and they invested the time to do well on it. State tests, on the other hand, are not a point of pride to a student as is the piece of art he stayed up late into the night to get just right, or the science project the student and her other team members created and presented to the class, which showed genuine admiration for the team's work. Not all celebration need come from the whole class or even be public, however; it can be private, taking place on the margin of the page, after class is over, or with the slightest nod of the head to which you might add a secret thumbs-up and a smile. The point is that when work is worth doing, it is worth celebrating, not just the predictable success of your best students, but the moments of wonder, which are sometimes as subtle as an idea or as humble as a single sentence written with grace and insight. Here, then, are some ways you can celebrate students' success in your class, and do so in ways that make a difference:

Be specific when celebrating individual, group, or class success, so that students know what they did that was so special; generic praise such as "Good job!" while welcome words to a few, is empty and offers nothing they might use to guide them on future performances. Instead, try saying something like, "I really appreciate the way your question opened up new connections in the discussion today."

Communicate praise to students, their classmates, in sincere, authentic ways via spoken and written comments (through notes, comments in margin, e-mail). You can also honor a student's success by referring to his or her work in class discussions, even if that student is not in class. Trust me, word will get back to them, and mean all the more. Also, recognizing success outside of the class—on the field, the stage, around the campus, in the community—will translate into good will and greater success *inside* the classroom. I often send an e-mail or write a quick note on an index card; also, I am glad to stop and have a personal conversation in the hall with a student I have not seen for a while or about whom I am worried.

Display, publish, or feature student work in class, around school, online (e.g., class or school Web site), or through a student anthology.

Acknowledge students as the source of good ideas you or others bring up in class. For example, you might say, "Ernesto raised some questions when discussing this idea with his group this morning and I thought we should take a look at what he said." Such efforts show that you listen to and remember what your students say and honor their intelligence and effort.

Ask students to explain their process to the class—the way in which they arrived at their elegant result; or, if you teach language arts, invite students who distinguished themselves to read their poem or story aloud to the class.

Keep in Mind Everyone desires praise and celebration, some recognition of his or her effort and ideas. But not everyone welcomes it in front of an audience. In some cases, it can bring on harsh treatment from others in the class who feel that the student made them look bad. In other situations, the student may want to learn and succeed but cannot afford to show it to his friends, and so any public recognition threatens to "blow his cover" by showing that he actually cares. The more you know your students, the better you know what they need. For some, I pass a note or make a comment after class; for others, I put their work on the overhead as an excellent example to others but leave the name off, perhaps even typing it up to make it more anonymous; but the person who did it knows it is theirs and will appreciate the recognition—and the consideration you showed him or her.

Curriculum Basics

7. Teach Skills and Knowledge in Context

Skills and knowledge offer solutions to problems we face; to the extent that these skills and this knowledge are useful to us, we are motivated to acquire them. Through a simulation called the China Game, students at my school were able to experience the daily changes of fortune that affected people during the rise of Communism in China. A range of experiences obviously requires more than one instructional approach: some skills are best taught through direct, explicit instruction; other ideas and skills are better taught through simulation and more active learning methods; and some benefit from the integration of the two for deeper, more robust learning to take place. Each type of instruction, however, has its place.

Regardless of the type of instruction, you know that learning exists along a continuum of mastery. Thus, you cannot hope for students to remain anything but novices if instruction is always decontextualized. My 15-year-old son clearly wants to learn to dribble the basketball better, but he realizes he won't become a better player if he doesn't put the skills to use in a real game. To develop the fluency and mastery your students require, they must work in ways that develop their ability to solve increasingly difficult problems that may take more time, and thus more patience and analytical thinking. Such thinking can only be achieved through application, which develops the independence students need if they are to succeed in class, on tests, and out there in the world.

Guiding Principles

1. Design authentic learning experiences that integrate skills and knowledge.

2. Use different types of instruction to teach skills and knowledge.

3. Develop fluency through variation within lessons.

4. Organize instruction into patterns for maximum effectiveness.

5. Teach a range of skills and types of knowledge.

Design authentic learning experiences that integrate skills and knowledge.

Robert Sternberg (1999) argues that "children develop expertise in the skills needed for academic tests as well as expertise in skills needed in real-life experiences" through "purposeful, engaging experiences [which] add to the acquisition process."

The following suggestions will help you integrate skills and knowledge when designing learning experiences:

Embed skills and knowledge instruction within the context of an authentic, purposeful assignment such as writing a play, letter, speech, or research paper; solving a problem in science, health, or economics; designing or constructing a project in shop, science, or mathematics.

Have students identify and solve problems they encounter in the context of their work by teaching them the steps in the problem-solving process: identify a problem by asking, "What's the problem here?"; define the problem by asking, "What are the components of the problem?"; formulate a problem-solving strategy by asking, "How can this problem be solved?"; allocate resources, asking "What is needed to solve this problem?"; and evaluate the solution, asking "Was the problem solved successfully?" (Astleitner 2005).

Jim Burke

Organize the learning experience around essential questions that drive inquiry and create a context for teaching new skills and knowledge. In my senior English class, for example, students spend much of the first semester reading a variety of texts as they explore the questions, "Who am I?/Whose am I?" which also creates a useful context to teach argument, literary devices, and reading strategies. After first reflecting on the question and how it applies to themselves, we use it to explore the questions as they relate to Hamlet, who spends most of the play trying to figure out who he is.

Ask yourself, "What do I want students to know and be able to do at the end of this activity and at the end of the semester? And what, then, is the most effective means by which my students might learn that?" In my freshman English class, for example, I want students to be able to find their own books, use those books to examine a topic from different perspectives, and synthesize all that learning in a paper with proper citations and quotations that support a central idea about the subject they studied.

Design learning experiences using context-rich activities such as simulations, case studies, performances, investigations, projects, and productions. A social studies teacher I once worked with, taught students through simulations of other cultures' activities; so, for example, when studying India and its local governing structures, called *panchayats*, he would have students take different roles and conduct a panchayat, then discuss its principles and how they differed from our own here in America. Such activities often require careful preparation, including time to rehearse what to say and create a dramatic environment.

Use different types of instruction to teach skills and knowledge.

In her landmark study of adolescent literacy, Judith Langer (1999) studied "beat the odds schools," guided by the question, "What did they do to achieve such consistent success?" While the study focused on middle- and high-school literacy, the findings are, at their heart, about effective instruction. To put it another way, what are we trying to accomplish in any of our disciplines if not some form of literacy? Langer identified three distinct types of instruction, each of which has its place on the instructional menu: separated, simulated, and integrated. *Separated* instruction, Langer writes, "is what most educators would consider to be direct instruction of isolated skills and knowledge." By definition, separated instruction is ancillary to the larger assignment, which requires that students possess certain discrete skills or knowledge. Separate instruction includes such content as rules, procedures, specialized vocabulary, facts, or conventions.

Once students have learned the skill or knowledge, they must put it to use. Otherwise, the learning will quickly wither and vanish, as a language does if we do not continue to speak or read it. Thus, *simulated* instruction asks students to *use* those rules and conventions, words and procedures, within the larger context of an assignment. Langer explains that she chose the word *simulated* "because the tasks themselves are specially developed for the purpose of practice."

The third type, *integrated* instruction, requires students to "use their skills and knowledge within the embedded context of a large and purposeful activity, such as writing a letter, report, poem, or play for a particular goal (not merely to practice the skill) or planning, researching, writing, and editing a class newspaper." Langer concluded that "*separated, simulated,* and *integrated* activities can all occur when needed within the ongoing instructional program," whereas ineffective schools favor one or two of the approaches over the other. Here are some ways you can incorporate different types of instruction into your class:

Ask yourself what skills you should teach through separate instruction before you begin a major assignment, read a text, or work on a new problem. An English teacher, for example, prior to having students write a persuasive essay, might explicitly teach (or review) the elements of an effective argument.

Offer opportunities to practice and apply the skills and information before students begin (or continue with) the main assignment. If, for example, you are teaching students how to cite sources on a research paper, you might do a mini-lesson on how to cite the specific types of texts and resources students have been using.

Evaluate the assignment—project, performance, or product— for essential background knowledge you should teach through direct instruction. A social studies teacher, for example, might front-load certain terms and information about the Depression before beginning to teach it.

Stop throughout the larger activity or assignment to address, through separate and simulated instruction, the specific skills and knowledge students need for the next step or which their current performance on the assignment suggests they do not yet understand fully. On a research paper, for example, students may need guidance in how to choose, use, and cite quotations effectively in their paper, or paraphrase those passages they do not want to cite.

Jim Burke

Provide meaningful, authentic opportunities to use and improve upon skills and knowledge that show what they have learned and allow them to extend their skills and knowledge through independent and more advanced application. In addition to writing actual research papers, students might reduce these down to three-minute presentations to learn or reinforce their public speaking skills.

Develop fluency through variation within lessons.

Years ago, while living in Tunisia, I had to learn to speak Arabic, a beautiful but difficult language to learn. It was important that I become fluent, however, because I was going to teach local special education students for two years in Arabic. Returning for a moment to Langer's three types of instruction, I spent the mornings engaged in separate and simulated activities, learning everything from how to make specific sounds (that were very unnatural to my American mouth) to how to use certain words. In this controlled environment of the classroom, where words were spoken carefully, precisely, slowly, we did fine and felt some initial competence. It was only when we left school, however, and entered the city to find lunch or go to the café to get coffee that we realized how much more complex the language was: accents, speed, omissions, unfamiliar words, tenses, local idioms, and much more combined to make us feel our ignorance. Each day, after a lunch of humility on the streets, we would run back to the classroom to share our stories, ask endless questions, and beg for help. At night, exhausted, we urged our teachers, with whom we had to live, to speak to us in English, but they never would, smiling instead, and saying in Arabic, "I'm sorry, Mr. Jim, what did you say? I didn't understand you. Arabic only, please."

Slowly, however, we moved from words to simple sentences; and from these simple sentences to greater fluency of the language thanks to, in my case, hours spent in cafés listening, talking, asking—and blushing, for most mistakes seemed to somehow be very embarrassing. Soon enough, school was over and we all moved into our own towns, where we started schools, conducting all our business in Arabic, and living hours away from anyone else who could speak our own native language. Fluency was the inevitable result, though it came only through hard work and the patience needed to immerse myself in the greater complexities of the language that I needed to master if I was to sound more knowledgeable than a third grader. This same process—of moving through the simple and into the complex, from the beginner to the fluent user or speaker—applies to your own subject, to the lessons you want your students to learn. Regardless of the subject, what you most want is that your students be fluent in your subject, to read, write, speak—to think—like a scientist, historian, author, mathematician, and so on. The following techniques offer some guidance in how to achieve this fluency:

> **Add complexity as students begin to show initial mastery** on formative assessments, varying the level of difficulty as you go to improve dexterity with the material or the skills students are learning. One obvious way to do this is to arrange problems related to the subject you're teaching, from easiest to most difficult. Whether it's grammar or algebraic problems, Italian sentences or scientific problems, students develop confidence and intellectual fluency when each problem is more difficult than the one that preceded it.

Vary the means and materials students use, as well as the configurations within which they work to increase fluency and flexibility. Students should know, for example, how to communicate the same message in 3,000, 300, and 30 words, all with equal effect. So, too, should they know how to convey the same information by writing, speaking, or creating multimedia products, such as videos.

Increase the complexity or difficulty by adding new elements to the problem, giving students additional directions that amount to more cognitive balls to juggle. When working on a paper, for example, it is helpful and challenging to ask students to trim 100 words from the essay in order to learn the value of concision in writing.

Vary the duration of the activity or exercise, asking students to work at different speeds to improve not just fluency but speed and stamina, two capacities that are essential to success in certain academic situations. Some timed writing activities, for example, help students become adept at quickly generating ideas and writing coherently about a text or topic.

Support your students in a variety of ways. Early on, a math teacher might offer more guided instruction, modeling a few problems and then asking kids to try. As fluency emerges, students can do the work on their own, reflecting in words afterward about the choices they made, what strategies helped the most.

Organize instruction into patterns for maximum effectiveness.

"Teaching is a system," argue Stigler and Hiebert (1999), a conclusion they drew from analyzing mathematics instruction in different countries around the world. Focusing on three countries—Germany, Japan, and the United States—they noticed recurring features within countries, for example, the way all Japanese teachers would begin class or discuss a problem. Such patterns "define different parts of a lesson and the way the parts are sequenced."

The German Lesson	The Japanese Lesson	The U.S. Lesson
Four activities characterize the German lesson: • Review previous material . • Present the topic and the problems for the day. • Develop the procedures to solve the problem. • Practice.	Five activities characterize the Japanese lesson: • Review the previous lesson • Present the problem for the day. • Have students work individually or in groups • Discuss solution methods. • Highlight or summarize the major points.	U.S. lessons follow a sequence of four activities: • Review previous material • Demonstrate how to solve the problem of the day. • Practice. • Correct seatwork and assign homework.

Stigler and Hiebert (1999). One key difference is that U.S. lessons devote more time to "practicing definitions and procedures and less time to developing details and rationales for procedures."

The point here is not which pattern best describes your teaching or which one is "best" (though the authors strongly favor the Japanese instructional model when it comes to math) but rather that there *is* a pattern to how we teach, one that Stigler and Hiebert argue is culturally based, a result of not only your teacher training program but 13 years of acculturation through your own schooling. Thus, the important idea is to identify the pattern your instruction follows and evaluate its effectiveness and how it might be improved. Try the following ideas to help you analyze and refine your instructional pattern:

Analyze your class over several days to identify the instructional moves you make, when you make them, how long each one lasts, and why you organize your instruction into those steps, that sequence. After doing this in my own class, for example, I realized that I tend to lead with a short, focused piece of instruction (e.g., how to make predictions). We then practice and then apply the learning to the main text we are studying and then we move into a writing assignment or structured discussion that ties it all together.

Identify the verbs that characterize the different stages of your instructional pattern, evaluating each one in light of its intended and actual effect. One sequence I found common to most classes is: generate, evaluate, analyze, organize, and synthesize. In a history class, for example, students might generate causes and effects of the movement, then evaluate which are most important, then analyze how these few events culminated in the movement.

Compare your own pattern with other teachers you respect, asking them if you can observe their class for a day or more to study their pattern.

Evaluate the language you use to set up, teach, and explain your curriculum, realizing that this is a crucial but less visible element of your teaching pattern. In working with student teachers, for example, I have noticed that they often don't explain how they want students to do an activity, perhaps because they are so focused on remembering what to do. Next time, try using an equation like this to explain: Today we are going to do A for these reasons, and will do it this way, because.... So let me get started by first showing you what I mean...

Examine the time you spend on each element of the pattern, asking yourself if this is an appropriate and effective amount that adds up to a balanced instructional pattern. Some teachers, for example, spend an inordinate amount of time on vocabulary at the expense of the larger curriculum and thus undermine the effectiveness of their teaching.

Teach a range of skills and types of knowledge.

Astleitner (2005) argues that "basic knowledge" consists of two main types: declarative and procedural. Declarative knowledge includes facts, concepts, and other such background knowledge needed to complete a larger task, solve a problem, or understand a text. The second type, procedural knowledge, includes rules and conventions, the knowledge of how to follow certain techniques and use tools. Consider the following suggestions when teaching a range of skills and knowledge:

Ask yourself what skills, of any type, are necessary to do what you ask. If, for example, you ask students to generate, evaluate, or analyze—three examples of what Sternberg calls "thinking skills"—you should ask whether they know how to do that (or do it the way, or at the level, you expect).

Model and incorporate these different types of skills for students, showing them not only how to do them but that you, and others in different fields, use them as well. When talking about how to read literature, for example, I often narrate my reading, telling them how I evaluate the importance of details and use these to make inferences about character or tone in the text.

Monitor the skills and knowledge you have taught
students lately and, if you find that you are repeating
yourself or not moving to higher levels in these areas,
reevaluate your instructional practices and assumptions.
When teaching a series of short stories, for example, it can
be easy to use the same techniques repeatedly, forgetting
that students need to use new tools or techniques to reach
higher levels of critical thinking.

Post certain declarative and procedural knowledge
on the board or poster paper for easy reference
throughout an activity that might require such skills
and knowledge. Keeping this information ever present
helps make it an easily accessible part of the students'
memory. In a biology class, for example, the teacher
might post the fundamental questions scientists use
when conducting experiments and tell students to use
that poster as a guide.

**Move beyond basic knowledge into such advanced,
critical thinking** as analysis and evaluation of problems,
texts, or techniques. When working with average kids, it
can be easy to assume that they cannot go higher than
comprehending the story or article you read; yet I find that
if given the tools to help them do so, students can always
do more analytical, advanced work on such texts. For
example, cause-and-effect analysis is pretty advanced, but
if given an organizer to direct their attention to the right
parts of the text, students begin to see how these elements
contribute to the meaning of the text.

8. Organize Your Instruction Around Big Ideas and Essential Questions

The very word *question* suggests an engaging, real purpose: one goes on a *quest* to discover a place, a person, a solution, something that helps to answer a larger, even more profound question. Schools exist for the very purpose of helping both students and teachers answer these big ideas and essential questions. The great biologist E. O. Wilson once said in an interview that no one comes into his class wanting to know about the cell, so he begins his course by asking them, "'Is sex necessary?' which is a question they all respond to and must discuss the cell in order to answer."

Guiding Principles

1. Use essential questions and big ideas to frame and guide your instruction.

2. Connect materials and assignments to the big ideas and essential questions.

3. Include the characteristics of effective curriculum in your conversation.

4. Create coherence and continuity within and across conversations.

5. Consider ideas and questions from different perspectives.

Use essential questions and big ideas to frame and guide your instruction.

Big ideas and essential questions are the engines that drive real learning. They transform a passive class into a community of active learners engaged in the quest to discover answers—their own and others'—to questions we have never stopped asking. Often the essential question begins as a topic the class will study. Students might enter the American history class one day and find the subject "War" written on the board, which is merely the beginning; the questions they might generate could lead to an essential question, such as "Is war necessary?" or "Is there such a thing as a just war?" With these questions—which can be posed before, during, or after—to light the way, the class will have a useful framework within which to work and think as they read, write, view, research, and discuss the subject. Embedded within this inquiry will be important opportunities to teach specific skills and background knowledge needed to answer the question.

In *Understanding by Design* (2005), Wiggins and McTighe looked closely at the notion of essential questions. They argue that a question is an essential question if it is intended to:

1. Cause genuine and relevant inquiry into the big ideas and core content.

2. Provoke deep thought, lively discussion, sustained inquiry, and new understanding, as well as more questions.

3. Require students to consider alternatives, weigh evidence, support their ideas, and justify their answers.

4. Stimulate vital, ongoing rethinking of big ideas, assumptions, and prior lessons.

5. Spark meaningful connections with prior learning and personal experiences.

6. Naturally recur, creating opportunities for transfer to other situations and subjects.

How can you use all these ideas to formulate your own essential questions? Here are some suggestions:

Identify the core subject of the discussion, lesson, unit, or course. In a history class, the subject could be an idea, like revolution, or a specific instance, such as the American Revolution.

Create an essential question about this big idea or core subject. My wife, a wonderful social studies teacher, organized a unit around the essential question, "Is war ever just?"

By yourself or with your students, generate many possible big ideas related to this core subject. Sticking with the previous example of a just war, the social studies teacher might, with her students, come up with such essential questions as, "What is one's obligation to his or her country during war?"

Post your big idea or essential question on the board, Web site, or classroom wall and return to it regularly. The history teacher could, for example, set up a blog to which she and her students could post new ideas and links as they explore this "just war" question over time.

Revisit and refine your essential question as new questions arise, new discoveries unfold, and new information comes in from ongoing research, discussions, and reading. Returning to our running example here, the history teacher might revise the question, in light of the class discussions, to "*When* is war justified?"

Tech Note! Consider creating a blog or threaded discussion about your big idea or essential question. Students can post their thoughts and responses to remarks made by you and others as the unit unfolds. The Civil War might become an area of rich inquiry if you ask students to have an online discussion in which they compare America's Civil War to other wars, including the war in Iraq. Students and teachers could post links to news articles and other resources as they discover them.

Connect materials and assignments to the big ideas and essential questions.

It is not enough to formulate compelling questions about the big ideas in your class. Such ideas are, in the beginning, like a bridge that must lead somewhere; otherwise, without some sense of destination, your kids will be stuck at the end, looking over the brink of the unit, wondering where it all goes, what this was all leading up to. They need a sense of culmination, something that gives shape to all they learned along the way. In his book *Engaging Readers and Writers With Inquiry*, Jeff Wilhelm suggests three "basic steps for creating an inquiry-oriented classroom: (1) identify an essential question and associated enduring understanding; (2) identify a final project; (3) create a "backwards plan" (2007, 39). He defines a backwards plan as a "carefully ordered set of activities that support students' progress—text by text and activity by activity—toward their ability to complete the final project independently." It is these "final projects" that show what students have learned and create opportunities for you to teach the standards you need to teach. Consider these suggestions for ways to make these connections in your classroom and curriculum:

Arrange a set of texts—nonfiction, fiction, poetry, Web sites, films, graphics, artwork, and more—that examine the subject of your inquiry from as many perspectives as possible. An art history teacher, for example, might, instead of studying work by period, examine it by topic; thus, she might have her students examine the depiction of beauty, for example, across eras and genres, and supplement the art with critical readings. Another might pair poems and paintings, asking students to study the different ways of looking at the story of the fall of Icarus, for example.

Provide alternative experiences related to the inquiry, such as guest speakers, WebQuests, or field trips. The art history teacher previously mentioned could easily arrange for a WebQuest or field trips for a closer look at the material.

Organize the class into groups, each with a different aspect of the inquiry to examine and then share with the class. For example, my colleague Morgan Hallabrin has groups of sophomores, as part of a inquiry into why people were silent during terrible times, study different tyrants, whom they then relate to the characters in *Lord of the Flies*.

Give students the choice from Wilhelm's (2007) three categories of "meaningful-making projects": formal writing, multimedia compositions, and social action projects. Students in one high school, for example, used literature circles to examine different groups in society, one of which was people with disabilities. The unit—which sought to explore the topic through interviews, articles, films, and a novel—culminated in a service learning project at a local service center for people with disabilities and a subsequent paper reflecting on the essential question based on their reading, discussions, and experience.

Keep returning to the essential question you have posted on a poster or a wall, adding comments, questions, associations, and new connections as the work unfolds.

Include the characteristics of effective curriculum in your conversation.

We love those days when the classroom is on fire with ideas, everyone is contributing to the discussion, and new connections are flying around like sparks. Yet the great conversation of one period somehow doesn't happen with the next class, or any other period that day. Good instruction shouldn't be an accident. It should be designed, achieved through careful planning that takes into consideration not only your students, but the material you are teaching. Here are some suggestions:

Choose materials from a range of perspectives and sources that will support extended and meaningful conversations, but which students will have time to explore and discuss in depth.

Jim Burke

Provide the support students need in order to enter into and contribute to these conversations.

This may mean giving students specific language in the form of sentence starters or modeling for them how to discuss certain material. In my AP literature class, for example, students often do not know how to engage in higher-level discussions of literature, so I will put on the board phrasings like: Who did what to whom, for what reason—and so what? The author did x in order to achieve y.

Show that you expect all students to have good ideas
to contribute to the conversation, by soliciting their ideas,
giving them time to develop the ideas, and helping them
generate ideas through modeling what you expect. The
government teacher, for example, might have students
examine one of the more recent Supreme Court cases and
write a response to it in preparation for a class discussion,
using that writing as a guide.

**Choose subjects and texts that have some connection
to each other** and the big idea at the center of your
curriculum.

Create coherence and continuity within and across conversations.

Without coherence and continuity, your curriculum deteriorates
into a scramble of facts, a pile of pieces that don't fit together in
any coherent, meaningful way. Here are some suggestions for ways
to create or maintain a coherent curriculum:

Ask yourself what subject or question is at the center
of your curriculum when planning and how does this
activity, text, or experience relate to it?

Keep a running narrative of connections and ideas
on the board during the class, allowing you and your
students to refer back to what you were doing or
discussing earlier in the unit or lesson.

Provide time for students to reflect on what they know
or have learned and, if time allows, invite students to
share their ideas in group or class discussions. I try to
use time at the end of the period, for example, to have
students write about what we did that day.

Begin with the end result in mind and, using that as an
objective, design your instructional sequence so it has a
logic to it; keep in mind the big ideas and essential skills
you want students to learn along the way in the context
of the larger instructional goal.

Connect the current conversation with previous units and the content of other classes when appropriate, to create a greater sense of coherence across subject areas or within your own class. When the health teacher begins teaching the unit on healthy eating, it provides an opportunity to return to the overarching theme of making the right decisions, a big idea the teacher introduced at the beginning of the semester and has returned to throughout units on sleep, drugs and alcohol, sex, and relationships.

Consider ideas and questions from different perspectives.

In today's global environment, students must develop the ability to consider a subject from different perspectives. The medium you use to explore a subject offers many angles of vision. A visual medium like video will inevitably differ from words on a printed page or a dramatic performance. By bringing in these different and sometimes conflicting perspectives, you teach your students not only to navigate their way through the real world, but hold in their mind conflicting ideas and retain the ability to function, something Scott Fitzgerald said was the true measure of a person's intelligence. Here are a few suggestions for how to teach students to consider an idea from different perspectives:

Require students to come up with several ways to solve the same problem or interpret the same text; ask them to examine and explain the process by which they arrived at these alternatives. In a biology class, students studying evolution can create their own unique animal, explaining how its different features illustrate evolution. When they finish, the biology teacher could ask them to explain how they came up with the idea of a snake that, in their vision of the future, flies and eats birds.

Incorporate into your curriculum a range of voices on the same subject, in different media if possible. The American history teacher can bring in readings from the Harlem Renaissance along with excerpts from the

Ken Burns documentary *Jazz*, along with primary-source documents such as newspaper articles and journals.

Use a graphic organizer with a circle in the middle for the subject or essential question, and different slices radiating out. In each slice, students should take notes on what the different sources say about the subject or essential question you are trying to answer.

Ask students to consider how different groups— ethnic, cultural, gender, racial, economic—would explain or respond to an event, idea, or text. In a social studies class this might mean asking students to examine how different groups of people saw an event like the Holocaust or how different groups would respond to certain economic policies. In a science class, it could involve asking what ethical concerns might arise for different groups as part of a discussion about, for example, genetic engineering.

Bring different perspectives in through alternative versions of a text. In English, for example, I will have students read as many as four different translations of a particular scene in Homer's *Odyssey* comparing how each translator creates a different characterization of Telemachus, son of Odysseus.

Tech Note! The growing media universe provides a dazzling array of perspectives, some highly specialized and others entirely inappropriate. Look for opportunities to expand the array of perspectives through different media. I created a "digital textbook" www.englishcompanion.com/room82/weeklyreader.html to allow my students to do this.

9. Help Students Make Connections

Our brains are not unlike the old switchboard operators, in one key sense: Our brain, upon receiving new information, responds by thinking, "I'll connect you right now," to whatever you know or have experienced in the past regarding a particular subject. Unlike a switchboard, which was limited in the number of connections it could make, the brain has a virtually inexhaustible capacity to learn, thanks to its ability to detect patterns and make approximations, to self-correct and learn from experience by analyzing external data and reflecting on its processes, and to create without limits (Caine and Caine 1994, 3). In *Making Connections: Teaching and the Human Brain*, Caine and Caine wrote that the brain is predisposed to "search for how things make sense, to search for meaning in experience. This translates into the search for common patterns and relationships. It is a matter of finding out how what is being learned relates to what the learner already knows and values and how information and experiences connect" (4). The authors identify two key components of brain-based learning that have important implications for instruction: Teachers must design and orchestrate lifelike, enriching, and appropriate experiences; and they must [ensure] that students

Guiding Principles

1. Generate a variety of types of connections.

2. Help students make—and extend—connections.

3. Make relevant, appropriate, and timely connections.

4. Identify opportunities for possible connections when planning lessons or teaching.

5. Use connections to improve comprehension, increase engagement, and enhance memory.

process experience in such a way as to increase extraction of meaning" (8). Your job, then, is to figure out what those key connections are and design lessons that will help kids not only make them but learn how to do so on their own in the future.

Generate a variety of types of connections.

The most familiar connections involve making connections between the text and yourself, to other texts you have read or are currently reading, and to the world at large.

Connecting what students are learning to essential questions or big ideas, as mentioned, improves learning, motivation, and recall. For example, a social studies teacher and I had students study several different cultures in the midst of change. My colleague, Frank Firpo, had students make connections to the central question of how best to govern a diverse society, reading various texts and watching certain films. As the English teacher, I had them reading literature from these different countries, written in different eras and perspectives, all of which was chosen for its relationship to the essential question. Here are some other ways to include different types of connections:

Use graphic organizers, such as Venn diagrams, to show similarities and differences between different texts on the same subject. In a health class, for example, students make connections between their own diet and the diet of people from other cultures, organizing their findings in a Venn diagram, then synthesizing these into a piece of academic writing.

Generate questions individually or as a class, specifically designed to make connections of one type or another. In a history class, for example, students compare the French Revolution to both the American Revolution and, in more modern times, the Communist revolution in China. Or, in an English class, advanced students study the elements of tragedy, then make connections from different texts (e.g., *Oedipus, Antigone, Hamlet*) to these tragic elements and between the texts themselves.

Prepare study guides, anticipation guides, or advance organizers with questions that solicit different types of connections. When studying *Lord of the Flies*, for example, my students complete an anticipation guide made of examples they must define as evil or not, which serve to generate a working definition of what evil is and is not, which they can then apply to the novel.

Ask students to use some form of guided or structured note-taking strategy that requires them to make various kinds of connections while they read, discuss, or investigate. Students in a science class, for example, could use a three-column format for cause-and-effect notes, writing "Event (Cause)" atop the far left column, "Effect" in the middle, and "Implications" in the third.

Create a chart of the different types of connections students should be able to make and ask them periodically what other types of connections they might be able to make. For instance, after a discussion of text-to-text connections, you might ask them what connections they might make to the recent news about global warming or health trends, thereby challenging them to connect in-school knowledge with the world outside.

Help students make—and extend—connections.

While the brain naturally tries to identify patterns and make connections, academic subjects are not always intuitive. Making connections often requires some cognitive structure (e.g., comparing and contrasting) or language (e.g., *x* reminds me of *y* because of *z*) if students are to generate a meaningful connection they can articulate or that they can extend to reveal a deeper understanding. Marzano, Pickering, and Pollock (2001) found that "presenting students with explicit guidance in identifying similarities and differences enhances students' understanding of and ability to use knowledge" (15) as does asking students to do so independently. They also found that "identification of similarities and differences can be accomplished in a variety of ways," by using four different "forms: comparing, classifying, creating metaphors, and creating analogies" (16). Here are some other specific ways to help students make and extend connections:

Model for students how to make the kind of connections you want them to learn; this includes modeling the process and language you use, the questions you ask, then discussing the process in a way that they can understand and repeat. A health teacher, for example, makes a connection between the current unit on the brain and the previous unit on diet, writing an equation on the board—x causes y because of a, b, or c—that shows the linguistic format of the comparison she wants to make to how the brain and body respond to what we put in them.

Ask students to create different metaphors and similes to more accurately represent or extend their connections. What begins as a text-to-self connection (e.g., this character and I are different because…) can then evolve into a more sophisticated connection when you use a metaphor (e.g., Ophelia is a puppet in the hands of those around her).

Create a three-column poster with sentence starters students can use to make different types of connections like the one below. Then have students choose the one they like most and use that to write a response or formal paragraph.

World	Self	Other Texts/Lessons
__ is similar to ___, in that they both ____.	Though not exactly the same, that character/moment/event reminds me of when I _____.	Though not exactly the same, that character/moment/event reminds me of one in another text _____.

Make connections to tests by asking students to create sample test questions like those they might encounter on in-class or standardized tests. Extend this form of connection by asking them to create not only factual questions, but more advanced, analytical questions or even essay questions.

Use Web sites that foster the making of connections.
For example, a Web site at Emory University pairs poems with the paintings that inspired them, enabling students to compare and analyze the two. (www.english.emory.edu/classes/paintings&poems/titlepage.html)

Make relevant, appropriate, and timely connections.

Not all connections are created equal. We have all had the student who is quick to raise his hand with some "connection" he is eager to share, only to find it is some wild non sequitur, such as when Tony asked me, in the middle of discussing *Of Mice and Men*, "Mr. Burke, do you think Barry Bonds is really taking steroids?" Nor are we entirely innocent ourselves. Often, in an effort to bring some personal color to the content, we tell some story which, by the time we finish, leaves us—along with our befuddled students—wondering how we ever thought that it related to the subject at hand. The point is, if connections are to be effective, they must work, must serve some instructional purpose. Connections, like similes, must also be based on things we understand; otherwise they create confusion instead of clarity. Connections also need to happen at the right time, while the subject is at hand. The only exception might be if, while planning your class that night, you decide that the day's discussion revealed that students still do not understand. In that case, you might come in the next day and offer some new connections. Say, for example, you realize your students still do not understand the idea of supply and demand. You might come in the following day with a brief demonstration based on cards they played with as kids (e.g., baseball, Pokémon or Magic cards) in which you ask them why some cards are more valuable than others. Finally, it is essential to make connections between what students are learning and why it is important. Here are some other possible ways to make such connections:

Draw a continuum on the board with "Relevant" at one end and "Irrelevant" at the other, and hatch marks in between. As you or students raise possible connections, you can evaluate how relevant or appropriate they are, using this continuum, developing criteria as you go. As time goes on, you can fill in descriptors to help clarify and illustrate the different degrees of relevance or importance. In a biology class, for example, when teaching students to evaluate the connections between different elements, students could start by generating categories (e.g., color, movement, shape, texture, number) they could use to make possible connections between one slide and the next, or a collection of data from different stages in a process.

Teach students to ask themselves—by gently asking the question first yourself—how their connection relates to the point at hand, or why they think it is important. Such gentle challenges demand that students defend and elaborate on their connections, providing, if possible, examples or evidence to support their thinking. For example, in English a student might ask if there is any connection between kids today and Holden Caulfield in *The Catcher in the Rye*. I would then ask how that relates to the book we are studying, asking a series of clarifying questions that lead to the explanation that the student believes Salinger was offering a commentary on youth in society at large, which makes the book as relevant today as it was in its own historical context.

Create a three-column chart with "Past," "Present," and "Future" such as the one opposite. Add to it examples over time, then have students synthesize it in a piece of writing once it seems fairly complete. An economics teacher, for example, would have students make connections about work in our society to better understand how it has changed and is likely to change in the future.

The World of Work

Past	Present	Future (predictions)
• Little formal education needed • Greater emphasis on skilled and manual labor • Focus on local (American) production, creating jobs • Women have limited role in workplace (except during WWII)	• More formal education needed • Fewer manual labor jobs available (and those pay less than in the past) • Rapid rise in outsourcing of jobs to other countries and automation	• Return of work to American workers, but at lower pay • Increased knowledge of technology needed for any job • Rise in number of women in top positions based on increased numbers graduating from college

Keep in Mind We cannot discuss making connections without emphasizing the important opportunity to connect what students are studying to their own culture. At the same time, it is equally crucial to realize that when we make connections between one thing and another, we often assume certain experiences are common to all. Consider beforehand whether the connection you intend to make will be accessible and useful to *all* students; if not, ask them to come up with their own or choose a more familiar comparison.

Identify opportunities for possible connections when planning lessons or teaching.

We call them things like "teachable moments" or "windows of opportunity." Some must be created through carefully designed planning; others must be recognized, often in the heat of the moment. Both are important and valid, but only one can be planned for; the other often blindsides the teacher, raising unsettling and unexpected questions. Still, in the midst of that distress is the seed of a powerful question that students want to discuss, a connection they *need* to make between what you want to teach and they want to learn. In his observations of a high school English class, Intrator (2003) describes a teacher named Mr. Quinn, who touches briefly on the issue of language, and the use of the N-word in particular, when introducing *The Adventures of Huckleberry Finn* to his students, but tells them they will discuss the word later, in a subsequent class. The kids, however, are not having it; they immediately jump in to make connections to other books (e.g., *To Kill a Mockingbird*) and their own personal experiences (e.g., playing basketball with people of different races). Faced with this incendiary situation, Mr. Quinn "encouraged the kids to slow down and think," posing questions to help them clarify and extend the connections they were struggling to make in the heat of the discussion. On subsequent days, Mr. Quinn prepared connections he wanted them to make in advance. He brought in an article about a school where African-American parents wanted to ban *Huck Finn*, in order to make connections to the class's recent conversation about race as well as the discussions about the Constitution he knew were taking place in their American history class. Here are some suggestions to help you anticipate and prepare for such connections:

Consult the state standards for key instructional content in the material or unit you will teach, then plan to give special attention to those elements as they arise.

Evaluate the content for potential controversies, tensions, problems, or topics that lend themselves to important discussions about students' own lives, other material they have studied, or the world at large. When we read *Oedipus the King*, for example, there is a passage

in which the chorus speaks boldly to the people of Athens about the loss of faith in the gods; I use this as an opportunity to invite a discussion about the role of religion and faith in our own society and their individual lives. While such a discussion is always excellent, it is nonetheless fraught with potential tensions, which I must anticipate and be prepared to address.

Monitor class discussions or interactions, looking for those moments when students get fired up about some issue, event, or idea; try to help them work through those connections to arrive at a new understanding of the material. For example, one time in my English class we were discussing some novel and the action within it, when a student enthusiastically said to the class, "This is just like the stuff we were learning in biology this morning, isn't it?" My role then was to help him explain and elaborate upon that connection, which others did as well, resulting in a very rich exchange.

Bring in material from outside of class that invites powerful connections to what you already intended to teach. Incorporate this material—an article, a clip from a film or television program, a photograph—deliberately and carefully into your lesson, using it to help students make connections.

Assign specific students the role, whether in full-class or group discussions, of looking for and making connections for the class. Such students are responsible for raising questions about possible connections, which the class can then consider on its own.

Use connections to improve comprehension, increase engagement, and enhance memory.

At the end of the day (or the period!), we want our students to understand and be interested in, and remember what they study in our class. Returning for a moment to the analogy of the brain being like a switchboard, you can easily imagine that every time you help a student make a connection (and, in the process, teach her to make it herself in the future) she will understand and remember it better. A more modern comparison might be to compare your brain to the Internet: everything in there is linked, and the more you activate those links, the better you understand how to use the site, how to navigate your way around the Internet; what's more, the more you activate those same links, perhaps using them in different contexts, the better you remember them. Eventually, through this increasingly dense network of actual and conceptual links (e.g., connections) you see the smaller lines that tie ideas and information together and thereby grow the tree of knowledge inside your brain. When the brain makes these connections, when it figures things out, when it creates or recognizes new patterns, it lights up with pleasure, actually creating a chemical basis for key memories that makes them easier to retrieve. Thus, the more you allow students to connect what they know and care about to what you teach, the more pleasure they will find in your classroom. Here are some suggestions for ways to improve comprehension and memory, while also increasing motivation to learn and succeed:

> **Pose hypothetical questions that enable students to bring in what interests them.** For example, ask kids how someone (e.g., a historical figure, a character from a favorite novel or film) would respond to a certain situation, question, or problem.

Bring in film, music, and art so that students can examine how an idea can be treated in different times, by different people, in different media. I have shown my students five very different paintings depicting Ophelia's drowning, leading students to make connections between the paintings and the original text.

Offer questions you know will intrigue them and, ideally, create emotional responses. Questions based on similes can be especially effective. A health teacher could as part of a unit on viruses, pose the question, "How is MySpace like a virus?" or "How is a relationship like a dance?"

Invite kids to create dramatic interpretations and adaptations of historical events, literary texts, or interpersonal scenarios; as part of the process, they should explain how the people in the enactment relate to the subject or texts they are studying, to other material they have studied, or, to their favorite subject— themselves.

10. Design Lessons and Units for Maximum Learning and Engagement

Great lessons are designed, not found; created, not bought. They draw on your knowledge not only of the subject, but your students. The best lessons combine both art and science. Recent research has given us many insights into effective instruction, elements we can incorporate into lesson designs. Marzano, Pickering, and Pollock (2001) identified nine instructional strategies, all based on extensive research, which improve student achievement across content areas and grade levels. They are:

- Identifying similarities and differences.
- Summarizing and note taking
- Reinforcing effort and providing recognition
- Homework and practice
- Nonlinguistic representations
- Cooperative learning
- Setting objectives and providing feedback
- Generating and testing hypotheses
- Cues, questions, and advance organizers

The point is that when designing lessons, you must be deliberate, purposeful in your planning; otherwise, to quote *Alice in Wonderland*, "If you don't know where you are going, any direction will take you there!" I tend to sketch out the month ahead, blocking off the upcoming week in more depth, and carefully planning each day the night before, based on what happened that day. Janet Allen (2007) offers a useful structure that helps teachers create effective lessons:

Guiding Principles

1. **Focus on desired outcomes when designing instructional sequences.**

2. **Align your instruction and assessments with the appropriate standards.**

3. **Create lessons that will motivate and engage all students.**

4. **Cultivate independence through instructional practices.**

5. **Teach for understanding.**

> The purpose of this lesson is to help students learn to
> _____ in order to _____
> by using _____. I will know they have
> learned it when _____.

Design must always take into consideration the user, which in our case means the student. Motivation and engagement are crucial challenges for all teachers today, who face arguably the most diverse classrooms in our country's history. Cushman (2003) asked students what advice they had for teachers trying to plan effective lessons, lessons that would not only help them understand but motivate them to learn. While not all of their recommendations are specific to design, they all have implications for either the structure of the lesson or its content. Students recommend:

- Be passionate about your material and your work.
- Connect to issues we care about outside of school.
- Give us choices on things that matter.
- Make learning a social thing.
- Make sure we understand.
- Respond with interest when we show interest.
- Care about students and their progress.
- Help students keep on top of their workload.
- Show your pride in our good work.
- Provide role models to inspire us. (2003)

When Should We Do That?: A Planning Chart by Students

Time of Day or Year	A good time to...	A bad time to...
First week of school	• Give a quick quiz to see what students know • Get to know students • Tell students about you • Make rules with students • Introduce the semester	• Joke around; be too nice • Judge; yell • Assign homework (you're just getting used to school after summer)
First thing in the morning	• Have something active to wake people up • Discuss, not write	• Give a big test • Give a lecture • Have gym
Before lunch	• Give a lecture about something important • Do a fun activity; an educational movie, or an outdoor project • Have gym • Read and write	• Do activities that deal with food (makes you hungry) • Talk about disgusting stuff • Have major projects • Give a test • Have a long talk with a hungry student
After lunch	• Write • Give a test • Exercise, have fun, play games before working	• Give a lecture • Do physical activities (disagreement on this) • Do nasty projects like dissection
Last period	• Have discussions • Watch a serious movie • Do some group work • Have recreation or gym	• Have a test (not focused, ready to go home) • Give a load of homework (other classes have already given it) • Give a speech or a lecture

Beautiful day	• Have class outside • Do something educational in the park • Read or do activities outside	• Send students out alone • Stay in and watch a movie • Stay in the classroom • Read from a dull textbook
Day before a holiday break	• Have a makeup day • Write about different things students are doing • Have a party	• Give a major test • Start a new subject or project • Give homework
Day after a holiday break	• Review previous work and get into new subjects • Talk or write about vacation	• Give a test or quiz • Have homework due • Give a big project
College application deadline week	• Give time in school to help with applications	• Assign lots of homework • Give tests
During standardized tests	• Do quick prep reviews using games or old work • Bring snacks	• Give homework or projects • Give other tests
Senior spring	• Do free reading or writing • Do a senior project	• Introduce new topics • Give other tests
Last week of school	• Have parties and trips • Have performances, presentation, project exhibitions • Evaluate the course	• Give hard, new, serious work • Have an important test

Cushman (2003). From *Fires in the Bathroom*

Finally, effective lessons today must be aligned with the standards you are required to teach. While some see such requirements as obstacles or constraints, effective teachers follow these guiding principles to create lessons that are both standards-based and engaging.

Focus on desired outcomes when designing instructional sequences.

Backwards planning, which you have read about earlier, asks teachers to begin with the end in mind, then make instructional decisions that lead to that result. This approach asks you to evaluate what you want students to know, understand, and be able to do. It also asks you to consider what means will be most effective in achieving that end, as well as what evidence you are willing to accept that they have learned it. When using a literature textbook in my freshman class, for example, I must ask what "take-aways" I want for my students after they finish reading a collection of texts. I could say that the reading and what they learn along the way is justification enough; but that leaves learning to chance and provides no assurance of a meaningful, productive outcome. Thus, I begin by asking what I want the students to learn (about themselves, the world, the subject, the texts themselves, and such other areas as writing and grammar), then arrange the texts in the order most suitable to that end (e.g., from easiest to most difficult, but all related to the subject of survival). Part of my challenge is to create an instructional context that will allow them to explore the subject through a range of types of text; to that end, I transform the subject—survival—into an essential question that all the texts answer in different ways: What does it take to be a survivor? I look at a list of text types, like the one opposite, I can use to explore the subject, all of which will provide opportunities to teach them what I want them to know and be able to do.

When planning your own lessons, use the following suggestions to help you determine and teach the desired outcomes:

Provide a clear, defensible rationale that is educationally sound for any content you teach, and any activity students do. When teaching writing, for example,

I point out that the ability to write well is consistently identified as one of the biggest factors in success in professional fields.

Ask yourself how any given step in the instructional sequence relates to or will help to achieve the stated learning outcomes. Teachers often like to incorporate discussion, for example, but unless it serves a specific instructional purpose (e.g., to prepare them to write about the subject they have read about) it is unlikely to be effective.

Reinforce for students what you expect them to learn and be able to do and how these outcomes will contribute to their own success in school and life. When teaching students about argument, for example, point out to them that they are surrounded by people—on television, in newspapers, in political races, through advertisements—trying to persuade them to buy, believe, or do certain things; then make clear that only those who understand these techniques can defend themselves against such tactics.

> ### Text Types to Consider
> Critical/analytical texts
>
> Myths/tales
>
> Speeches
>
> Primary sources
>
> Informational charts, statistics
>
> Photographs, artworks
>
> Nonfiction texts
>
> Media: video, film, audio
>
> Short stories
>
> Poems
>
> Fiction

Align your instruction and assessments with the appropriate standards.

"To guide curriculum decisions... teachers must know about national, state, and local standards for student learning" (Darling-Hammond and Baratz-Snowden 2005). In what Zmuda and Tomaino (2001) call a "competent classroom," an effective teacher focuses on four components: essential questions, content standards and instructional objectives, assessments, and performance standards. . . [so that] every component of instruction interlocks with every other component, producing a classroom with a consistent sense of purpose and direction." Content standards "are fixed goals of learning that lay out what students should know and be able to do—the knowledge and skills essential to a discipline that students should learn;" performance standards, on the other hand, "inform the student as to what his or her work should look like. . . describe levels of performance and/or evidence that the content standards have been met". Such standards are, if not aligned with the assessments, simply noble goals instead of guiding lights for both you and your students. "Alignment is the degree to which expectations and assessments work together to improve and measure students' learning" (Wisconsin Center for Education Research 2007). Such knowledge has levels, which you can apply before, during, and after the lesson to improve the design of your lesson:

Level 1 *Recall and reproduction*: Are you asking students to learn facts, definitions, terms, or procedures they must simply recall?

Level 2 *Skills and concepts*: Are you asking students to actively process what they learn, transcending the simplicity of Level 1, by requiring that they "classify," "organize," "estimate," "make observations," "collect and display data," and "compare data"?

Level 3 *Strategic thinking*: Are you asking students to reason, plan, provide evidence, and generally think with greater complexity than they did in the previous levels?

Level 4 *Extended thinking*: Are you asking students to use what they have learned at the previous levels to make connections within the content area or across disciplines? Are you asking students to evaluate different approaches to the same problem, choosing the best solution? (WCER 2007, 3)

Lesson Planning Template

Lesson: _____

Class: _____ Period: _____

PLANNING

Frame the Lesson: Position the lesson within you, curriculum and your students' academic needs: _____

_____

Establish Skill Set: List specific instructional activities: _____

_____

Gather and Prepare: List the resources you'll need and suggestions for adapting lessons for your students: _____

_____

TEACHING

Teach the Lesson:
- Develop instructional language, moves, and prompts
- Subdivide lesson
- Identify discussion topics
- Provide tangible and concrete examples

_____

_____

_____

_____

_____

_____

_____

ASSESSING

Assess and extend:
- List strategies to provide extra support or extra challenge
- Assess understanding of lesson
- Reinforce and extend lesson

_____

_____

_____

Create lessons that will motivate and engage all students.

In *School Smarts: The Four Cs of Academic Success* (Burke 2004), I sought to answer a simple question: Who succeeds in school and why? Of the four key domains—commitment, content, competencies, and capacities—it was the first, commitment, that consistently emerged as most crucial. Others have found the same, emphasizing the importance of that emotional connection that allows students to lose themselves in their work, a feeling we all hope for but rarely achieve in our students. Smith and Wilhelm (2002) examined the literacy of adolescent boys and concluded there were four main principles related to engagement: "a sense of control and competence; a challenge that requires an appropriate level of skill; clear goals and feedback; and a focus on the immediate experience" (29). Focusing specifically on literacy, Turner (1997) identifies three related but different characteristics of instruction that promotes student engagement: "they provide opportunities for challenge and self-improvement, autonomy, and social collaboration" (187). When designing lessons, consider the following suggestions for increasing engagement and motivation:

Evaluate *why* you are teaching something: If you cannot provide a compelling rationale for the lesson that would appeal to your students, they are not likely to understand or be able to learn what you are teaching them. In my senior English class, for example, when introducing *Oedipus the King* and other tragedies, I show a clip from the documentary *Enron: The Smartest Guys in the Room*, which I use to raise the question of whether we still have tragic figures and tragedies in our world today. Without such connections, it seems as if we are studying 2,500-year-old plays about dead people who never existed except on the page, something that to most seniors seems a bit of a waste of time.

Consider *what* you are trying to teach: If it is not engaging or connected to larger questions and concerns your students have, it is unlikely they will engage or learn. Reevaluate the texts, problems, or activities you initially chose, asking if others would provide a more meaningful challenge to your students.

Examine *how* you are trying to teach: Evaluate whether the approach you are taking is effective in both preparing students to succeed and engaging them in what they are learning. If it is not effective, consider using a more collaborative or interactive process through which they can better understand and thus remember and use the content. Reading and taking notes on Shakespeare's sonnets is one way to work with Shakespeare, but I find I get much more engagement and better results when I have them get into groups, then give each group a transparency of the sonnet they must prepare to teach the rest of the class in a presentation the following day. This has the advantage of increasing engagement while providing me a more localized context within the groups to raise questions and teach them about Shakespeare's language, for example.

Remember *who* you are teaching: Consider the audience for your lesson and whether your content and approach are appropriate for these particular students. This particular class may need a more social, active, or innovative approach than past students. Solicit suggestions from them about how they best learn. In my freshman English class, for example, I noticed kids talking about MySpace and other online worlds. I asked them if they would like to use a threaded discussion to respond to the story we read instead of taking notes as we had done in the past. The result: increased engagement, more writing, and dynamic discussions both in class and online.

Think about *when* are you teaching: Evaluate the time of the day, the time during the period, and the point in the year when you are teaching certain content. Some periods during the day or times of year present special challenges. Some teachers lead with content that would be better used *after* an introductory or otherwise more engaging lesson. Revise the assignment or change the timing to increase engagement. For example, in my AP English class, I have students who come from as many as five different English teachers junior year, all of whom have their differences. I use the beginning weeks to create a workshop during which we read short stories and focus on creating a common vocabulary and set of practices for reading, discussing, and writing about literature. Putting this up front allows me to evaluate where they are and create a culture of expectations that will get them were they need to be.

New Teacher Note Many new teachers, eager to put to use all they learned in their credential program, jump straight to content in the first days without realizing the importance of establishing a relationship and helping students transition from summer into the new school year. The lesson they wanted to use that first day is, no doubt, a great lesson, but one that would be better if used a week or two later when students have settled in and, thanks to your efforts, developed a willingness to work for you.

Cultivate independence through instructional practices.

The training wheels need to come off some time. At some point, every student must go into the state test or even the real world and put to use what they have learned. They cannot bring you with them to work, nor will the state allow you to hold their hand as your students take the exit exam. Yes, at some point, all this instruction is supposed to lead to some autonomy, to the ability to read, write, think, calculate, and investigate all on their own, using what you have taught them as a guide. Vygotsky (1978) introduced such a notion long ago in his zones of proximal development (ZPD) model, which asserted that learners can learn difficult material if provided guidance through the early stages of the process en route to independent application. More recently, Pearson and Gallagher (1983) developed what they called the "gradual release of responsibility" model to capture the process a learner undergoes on the way to fluency in three stages: teacher regulated, supported practice, and student regulated. Wilhelm offers a variation on this process: I do/You watch → I do/You Help → You do/I Help → You do/I watch (2001, 11). Develop your students' independence by doing the following:

Provide appropriate and repeated demonstrations of the expected academic behavior, narrating what you are doing, how you are doing it, when you are doing it, and why—*as you are doing it.*

Give students tools and strategies to use as they make their initial efforts to learn the content or behavior. In a social studies class, for example, the teacher might use a tool like the KWL organizer when reading about material he thinks students should know something about, even if only through the movies.

Offer feedback—verbal, written, or visual—on their performance which they can use to refine their actions and strategies. When reading a stack of papers that are not final drafts (especially when I am pressed for time), I will keep a pad of paper handy and note common patterns of error and success in the writing. Instead of writing on each paper, I will come in and summarize, usually with illustrating examples I have copied to a transparency, and offer feedback collectively, through my remarks and examples.

Allow students to apply what they have learned as they choose; for example, after teaching students a variety of note-taking or reading strategies, allow them to choose which one is most appropriate for the current situation.

Realize that as students do more complex work, they will need further support before achieving the same independence they had with material at lower levels. The student who understood *Romeo and Juliet* as a freshman will need additional guidance and instruction when learning to read *Hamlet* as a senior, for the second is much more sophisticated than the first.

Teach for understanding.

Once the standardized test is over and the worksheet turned in, the question is: Do the students really understand what they have learned? One can write a ten-page research paper, write it in graceful prose even, and have no understanding of the subject. Skills and knowledge are the foundations on which such understanding is built, but they are not ends in themselves. Perkins (1998) distinguishes between them this way: "knowledge is information on tap. We feel assured a student has knowledge when the student can reproduce it when asked... And if knowledge is information on tap, skills are routine performances on tap. We find out whether the skills are present by turning the tap. To know whether a student writes with good grammar and spelling, sample the student's writing.... Understanding is the ability to think and act flexibly with what one knows. To put it another way, an understanding of a topic is a 'flexible performance capability' with emphasis on the capability.... Learning facts can be a crucial backdrop to learning for understanding, but learning facts is not learning for understanding."

When you visit the online iCan film festival created by the San Fernando Educational Technology Team at http://sfett.com/ you get a real sense of what understanding looks like. Here students show, through their videos, not only their understanding of how to use technology to craft a compelling short film, but their knowledge of rhetoric, narrative, and the subjects, such as poverty, the Iraq War, or eating disorders, that they are investigating. Such productions are the culminating result of lessons that not only demonstrate but develop understanding. Yet not all instruction must be so high-tech: one science teacher wanted to assess students' initial understanding of the concept of classification and so brought in the junk drawer from her kitchen at home, telling kids to sort through it and come up with a classification system that would account for everything in it. Having established where they were, she set about teaching them more sophisticated scientific systems, eventually giving them a taxonomy of critical features to use when classifying their subsequent findings in a research project (Perkins, 1998).

As this last example shows, teaching for understanding does not preclude using direct or guided instruction to teach the skills and knowledge students need for the "performance of understanding" (Perkins 1998, 42). Such performances create a more authentic context in which to teach such skills and knowledge, a context that makes the lessons more meaningful and the student more motivated for now they see the material as relevant, even urgent. My colleague Diane McClain, for example, uses her Soundtrack of Democracy unit on great American speeches to examine themes in American society that students explore in detail, all the while learning about rhetoric, grammar, style, and history. Such presentations develop students' understanding of these strategies and devices, these elements and skills, while at the same time providing an authentic context in which to demonstrate their own understanding, through performance, of these elements in their own speech.

You can teach the necessary skills and knowledge while also teaching for understanding if you:

Decide what you want students to understand, know, and be able to do before you begin the unit, spelling it out in clear language for yourself and your students. I try to include these outcomes on the handout for any significant assignment. Here is an example from an independent reading assignment in my freshman English class:

Objectives
This assignment is designed to:
- Improve your reading speed, comprehension, and vocabulary
- Expose you to a wider range of authors and subjects
- Develop your identity as a reader
- Help you explore a subject in some depth over the course of the semester
- Write an essay about one subject that draws from multiple sources

Make available a range of possible means for students to demonstrate their understanding including, but not limited to, portfolios, performances, productions, or problems solved. When I have students with certain types of learning difficulties, I will allow them to meet with me and discuss a book they read instead of writing about it under the pressure of time.

Ask students to demonstrate their degree of understanding by first performing or producing some appropriate task, then analyzing it through verbal or written annotations in which they identify the different elements of, for example, an effective argument, where they used them, how, and why.

Return to these big ideas, understandings, and essential questions throughout the unit, semester, and even the year, instead of treating the curriculum as a linear experience. Such recursive teaching reinforces and deepens understanding.

Analyze the "performance of understanding" for key skills and knowledge found in the state standards and provide overt instruction and assessment of those areas, connecting them to the larger ideas contained in the unit. In English, this might mean looking at the different possible organizational patterns by which one might convey information and deciding which one (or two) are most appropriate to this assignment, then teaching students how to apply these skills and knowledge in this context.

Works Cited

Allen, J. (Personal conversation, July 28, 2007).

Applebee, A. (1996). *Curriculum as conversation: Transforming traditions of teaching and learning.* Chicago: University of Chicago.

Applebee, A. and Langer, J. (2003). Discussion-based approaches to developing understanding: Classroom instruction and student performance in middle and high school English. *American Educational Research Journal,* Vol. 40, No. 3, 685–730.

Astleitner, A. (2005). Principles of effective instruction—general standards for teachers and instructional designers. *Journal of Instructional Psychology,* Vol. 32, 2005.

Bain, Ken. (2004). *What the best college teachers do.* Cambridge, MA: Harvard University Press.

Bransford, J. D., Brown, A. L. , and Cocking, R. R. (Eds.). (2000). *How People Learn: Brain, mind, experience, and school.* Washington, D.C.: National Academy Press.

Burke, J. (2001). *Illuminating texts: How to teach students to read the world.* Portsmouth, NH: Heinemann.

Burke, J. (2005). *ACCESSing school: Teaching students how to achieve academic and personal success.* Portsmouth, NH: Heinemann.

Burke, J. (2004). *School smarts: The four Cs of academic success.* Portsmouth, NH: Heinemann.

Burke, J. (2007). *50 essential lessons: Tools and techniques for teaching English language arts.* Portsmouth, NH: Heinemann.

Caine, R. N. and Caine, G. (1994). *Making connections: Teaching and the human brain.* Menlo Park, CA: Addison-Wesley.

Cooper, H. (2001) Homework for all—in moderation. In *The best of educational leadership 2000–2001,* 31–35.

Costa, A and Kallick. (2000). *Activating and engaging: Habits of mind.* Alexandria, VA: Association for Supervision and Curriculum Development.

Cushman, K. (2003). *Fires in the bathroom: Advice for teachers from high school students.* New York: New Press.

Darling-Hammond, L. and Baratz-Snowden, J. (Eds). (2005). *A good teacher in every classroom: Preparing the highly qualified teachers our children deserve.* San Francisco, CA: Jossey-Bass.

Echevarria, J., and Graves, A. (2003). *Sheltered content instruction: Teaching English-language learners with diverse abilities.* Boston: Allyn and Bacon.

Freeman, D. and Freeman, Y. : *English Language Learners: The Essential Guide.* (2007). New York: Scholastic.

Gardner, H. (2006). *Five minds for the future.* Cambridge, MA: Harvard Business School Press.

Gardner, H. (1999). *The disciplined mind: What all students should understand.* New York: Simon and Schuster.

Gee, J. P. (2003). *What video games have to teach us about learning and literacy.* New York: Palgrave.

Graham, S. and Perrin, D. (2006). *Writing next: Effective strategies to improve writing of adolescent middle and high school.* Washington D.C.: Alliance for Excellence in Education.

Guskey, T. R. (2005). Mapping the Road to Proficiency. *Educational Leadership.* 63 (3), 32–38.

Hirsch, E. D. (2006). *The knowledge deficit: Closing the shocking education gap for American children.* Boston, MA: Houghton Mifflin.

Intersegmental Committee of the Academic Senates. (2002) *Academic literacy: A statement of competencies expected of students entering California's public colleges and universities.* Sacramento, CA: Intersegmental Committee of the Academic Senates.

Intrator, S. M. (2003). *Tuned in and fired up: How teaching can inspire real learning in the classroom.* New Haven: Yale University.

Jensen, E. (2005) *Teaching with the brain in mind.* Alexandria, VA: Association for Supervision and Curriculum Development.

Johnson, S. (2005). Could it be that video games are good for kids? *Los Angeles Times.* 27 July, B13.

Kelley, T. (2005). *The ten faces of innovation: IDEO's strategies for defeating the devil's advocate and driving creativity throughout your organization.* New York: Currency.

Langer, J. (1999). Common instructional features in uncommonly successful English/language arts program." Spring 1999 *English Update Newsletter*, p. 6

Levine, M. (2006). Interview with Marge Scherer, "Celebrate strengths, nurture affinities: A conversation with Mel Levine." *Educational Leadership*. 64 (1) 8–15.

Marzano, R. J. (2000). *Transforming classroom grading*. Alexandria, VA: Association for Supervision and Curriculum Development.

Marzano, R. J. (2004). *Building background knowledge for academic achievement*. Alexandria, VA: Association for Supervision and Curriculum Development.

Marzano, R. J. and Pickering, D. J. (2005). *Building academic vocabulary: Teacher's manual*. Alexandria, VA: Association for Supervision and Curriculum Development.

Marzano, R. J. and Pickering, D. J. (2007). The case for and against homework. *Educational Leadership*, 64 (6), 74–77.

Marzano, R. J., Pickering, D. J., and Pollock, J. E. (2001). *Classroom instruction that works: Research-based strategies for increasing student achievement*. Alexandria, VA: Association for Supervision and Curriculum Development.

Moran, S., Kornhaber, M., and Gardner, H. (2006). Orchestrating multiple intelligences. *Educational Leadership*, 64 (1), 22–28.

Olson, C. B. and Land, R. (2007). A cognitive strategies approach to reading and writing instruction for English language learners in secondary school. *Research in the Teaching of English*, 41 (3), 269–303.

Palincsar, A.S., and Brown, A.L. (1984). "Reciprocal teaching of comprehension-fostering and monitoring activities." *Cognition and Instruction*, 1, 117-175.

Pearson, P. D., and Gallagher, M. C. 1983. The Instruction of reading comprehension. *Contemporary Educational Psychology* 8:317–344.

Perkins, D. (1998) What is understanding? In M. S. Wiske (Ed.) *Teaching for understanding: Linking research with practice*. San Francisco: Jossey-Bass.

Pink, D. (2006). *A whole new mind: Moving from the information age to the conceptual age*. New York: Riverhead/Penguin.

Smith, M. W. and Wilhelm, J. D. (2002). *Reading don't fix no chevys: Literacy in the lives of young men*. Portsmouth, NH: Heinemann.

Sternberg, R. F. (1997) *Successful intelligence*. New York: Plume.

Sternberg, R. F. (2006). Recognizing neglected strengths. *Educational Leadership*, 64 (1), 30–34.

Sternberg. R. F. (1999) Ability and expertise: It's time to replace the current model of intelligence. *American Educator*, 23 (1), 10–13.

Stigler, J. W. and Hiebert, J. (1999). *The teaching gap: Best ideas from the world's teachers for improving education in the classroom*. New York: Free Press.

Tomlinson, C. and Jarvis, J. (2006) Teaching beyond the book. *Educational Leadership* 64 (1), 16–21.

Tomlinson, C. (1999). *The differentiated classroom: Responding to the needs of all learners*. Alexandria, VA: Association for Supervision and Curriculum Development.

Turner, M. (1997) *The literary mid: The origins of thought and language*. New York: Oxford.

Vygotsky, L. (1978). *Mind in society: The development of higher psychological processes*. Cambridge, MA: Harvard.

Wheatly, M. (2002). *Turning to one another: Simple conversations to restore hope to the future*. San Francisco, CA: Berrett-Koehler.

Wiggins, G. and McTighe, J. (2005) *Understanding by design*. Alexandria, VA: Association for Supervision and Curriculum Development.

Wilhelm, J., Baker , T. N., and Dube, J. (2001). *Strategic reading: Guiding students to lifelong literacy 6–12*.

Wilhelm, J. D. (2007) *Engaging readers and writers with inquiry: Promoting deep understandings in language arts and the content areas with guiding questions*. New York: Scholastic.

Wisconsin Center for Education Research (2007). Aligning assessments and standards. Summer 18 (4).

Zmuda, A. and Tomaino, M. (2001). *The competent classroom: Aligning high school curriculum, standards, and assessment— A creative teaching guide*. New York: Teachers College.